WHEN COFFEE WAS A NICKEL

God's Blessings
Ardyce

WHEN COFFEE WAS A NICKEL

by

ARDYCE H. SAMP

RUSHMORE HOUSE PUBLISHING
1989

Published by
Rushmore House Publishing
Box 1591
Sioux Falls, South Dakota 57101

ISBN 0-9624593-0-5
Library of Congress Catalog Number 89-092279

ALL RIGHTS RESERVED

Copyright © 1989 by Rushmore House Publishing

FIRST EDITION
2nd Printing 1989
3rd Printing 1990
4th Printing 1995

Edited by Randy Califf
Cover design by Bob Natz

Printed by Pine Hill Press, Inc., Freeman, South Dakota
Manufactured in the United States of America

Dedication

To my wonderful husband, Elden, who also lived through the Depression/Dustbowl Days in South Dakota and helped supply background depicting this era of prairie life. His uncanny ability as a walking dictionary and his knowledge in editing were invaluable. He was my inspiration and support.

To our son, Rollyn, for his efforts in encouraging me to keep writing and our daughter, Cynthia, for her support. Also spurring me on to stay with the typewriter were my daughter-in-law, Karen, and son-in-law, Duayne, who were always politely anxious to read what I wrote.

My hope is that our grandchildren: Michael, Matthew, Rebecca, Elizabeth, Anthony, April and Daniel will learn something about life a half-century ago.

To my mother, Rosella Habeger, who remembers clearly when coffee was only a nickel and a nickel was a monetary treasure.

— Ardyce

Meet the Author . . .

Ardyce
Habeger
Samp

"When Coffee Was A Nickel . . . " is an important historic slice of life from an era referred to in history books as the "Depression/Dustbowl Days."

Reading a history book, one might get a statistical sense calculating the loss of thousands of farms and the decline of rural towns during this period. However, lost in that sterile account of history are the lives of the people who stayed on the land and in rural towns in the post-Depression period.

Without a book such as this, youth of the "video recorder, microwave oven, instant shoe polish age" may never have the opportunity to pay a brief visit to their heritage. And for many older readers, this is a chance to revisit their past.

Ardyce Habeger was born in Madison, South Dakota. She attended elementary school at Madison and Rutland, South Dakota and graduated from Wentworth High School. She is an alumnus of Eastern State Teacher's College (now Dakota State University). Since 1948, she has resided and raised a family in Flandreau, South Dakota with her husband, Elden, now a retired educator.

She was a freelance writer of food columns, news and feature stories from 1948-1976. Her food column, "On the Range," was a weekly feature of *The Sioux Falls Argus Leader* for 22 years. Another column "Country Cooking," appeared in several area newspapers.

During the intervening years, she worked in a family business and helped their son, Timothy, a scholar and magician, "Tim the Terrific," who fought a lifetime of illness with cystic fibrosis. After his death, in 1982, she resumed her writing career.

Ardyce is an annual contributor to the Dakota History Conference at Dakota State University also writing history and short stories for area publications. She is a regular monthly contributor to *The High Liner*, official magazine of the REA and has had several articles published in *South Dakota Magazine*. She has won awards for short stories in the General Federation of Women's Clubs writing contests and published short items in national magazines.

About the Artists...

"When Coffee Was A Nickel..." brings a whole new marketing concept to contemporary art.

The artists illustrating this book have captured in pictures a visual remembrance of the post-Depression/Dustbowl Days when the country school, Fourth of July, Saturday night on main street and Halloween were a part of everyday life.

These illustrations are available in print form commissioned under the direction of long time Western Art Gallery operator, Shirley Savage, Sioux Falls, South Dakota.

She has afforded an opportunity for these artists to merge their talent in both the printed word and through their art. Each brings a special talent to this book.

Barbara Coppock links the past with the present by preserving old buildings in her illustrations. Many of her subjects will be gone in a few years, but her work will preserve their memory. She has never had formal art lessons, yet she is a highly skilled professional. She comes by her interest in historic buildings, homesteads and ghost towns very naturally. Her mother's family were dairy farmers, and her father was a carpenter. The blending of these backgrounds combined with her artistic and illustrative talent makes these subjects a natural. Being chosen to help illustrate "When Coffee Was A Nickel," Barbara says, "Even though I am not a native of South Dakota, I have long admired this part of the country. I am honored to be able to help preserve these memories in the state's centennial year. The tools I chose in this task were the most basic. A piece of paper and a pencil seemed the only way to illustrate these stories of life in the hard years, when paints and brushes were beyond the means of most aspiring artists."

Barbara and her husband Bill make their home in Omak, Washington, but can also be found searching the Northwest for subjects. The resulting art is the product of their teamwork, with Bill making frames for Barb's paintings, drawings and etchings. Barbara's work is alive with an aura of authenticity that will set your mind reeling back in time. Her illustrations are featured on the cover of the book and on pages 16, 26, 34, 44, 54, 64. She is regarded as one of the country's emerging western artists.

Connie Savage Thiewes was born and raised in South Dakota. Presently living in Huron, South Dakota, her life has centered around art from a very early age. The appreciation of the simplistic beauty of nature was stimulated by her late father, Jim Savage, sculptor/artist. This being a continuing influence in her life, she strives for the quality of painting that is seen with the eye and felt with the heart. Each painting completed is the center of Connie's education. The basics of art were taught through the patience of her father and self-study. After working as a commercial artist for ten years, Connie decided to concentrate on her painting full-time. Wildlife, songbirds, wildflowers or still-lifes all display a certain feminism echoing the association of mother and child. Being a mother of two has helped to open the limits of her visions of the world. She feels fortunate to have the opportunity to explore her creative energies in such a way. Her illustrations appear on pages x, 10, 88. She carries on a great family tradition as a leader in western art.

Chad Sperlich is currently enrolled as a full-time student at South Dakota State University, pursuing a degree in electronic engineering technology. A native of Armour, South Dakota, Chad is a self-taught artist. A lifelong interest in drawing and painting was given a chance to develop during his four-year stint in the Air Force. In his off-duty time, he had the opportunity to explore different techniques and define his skills. One of his commanding officers, impressed by Chad's work, commissioned him to paint murals in the company barracks. While stationed in Japan, he received recognition for his illustrations by capturing top honors in several art contests in the Pacific area. While pursuing his engineering degree, Chad finds his art a way to escape the rigorous number-crunching and memorization of schoolwork. His subjects are influenced by his love of western themes and motifs. Several of his pieces were included in the 1989 issue of *Prairie Winds*, Dakota Wesleyan University's annual literary magazine. His illustration appears on page 78.

Contents

1. When Fruit Crates Were Free 1
2. The Valentine Prize 5
3. The Cupid's Arrow 11
4. The Birthday Surprise..17
5. April Fool in Country School..........................27
6. A Country Charivari..35
7. Gone With the Wind Romance 45
8. Homeless Hoboes 55
9. Harold Goes to School......................................65
10. Halloweens Past 73
11. Who's in the Hen House?...............................79
12. The Christmas Box..89

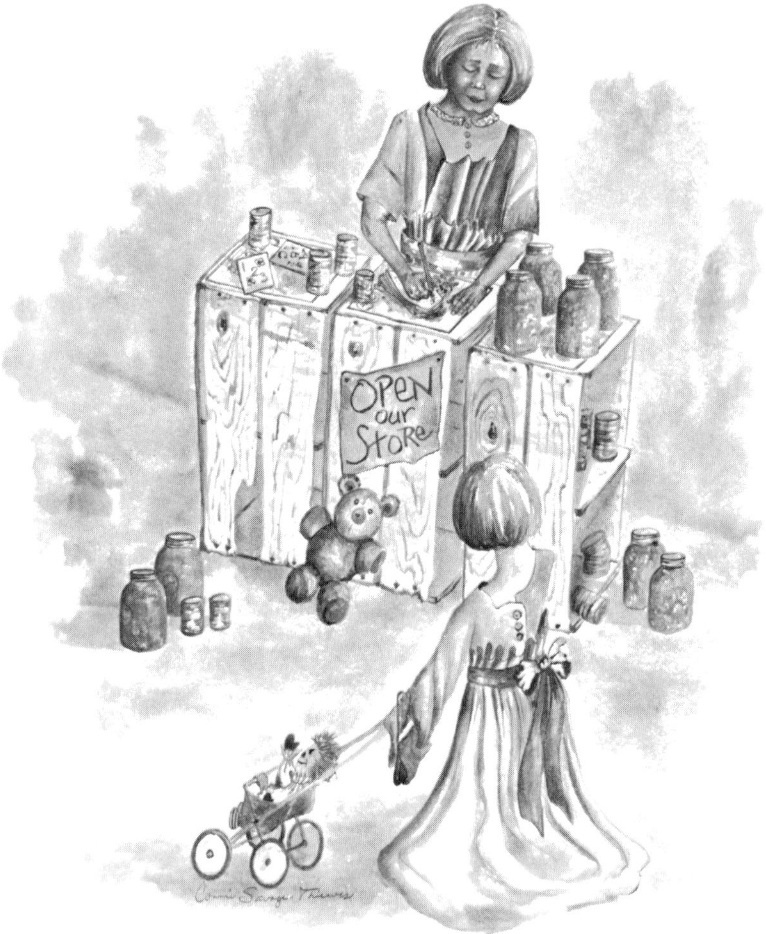
OPEN
our
STORE

When Fruit Crates Were Free

The Saturday TV shows were sports and rock music. The weather outside was a fright, and our eight-year-old grandson was visiting for the day. We knew he was bored before he declared, "There's nothing to do!" The toys we kept on hand for the grandkids were geared for toddlers or were things like a bat, ball, kits and books too hard for a second grader to read.

"What did you play with when you were my age?" Tony asked.

My mind raced back to childhood days spent on the farm, the "dirty thirties." There were three girls in our family. I was the oldest. We had to use our imaginations and anything at hand to fill our playtime, and we never ran out of things to do.

"Well, some Saturdays we played 'house' with the orange crates," I said.

"What's an orange crate?" asked our wide-eyed visitor. This sparked his interest as nothing else had that particular day.

"Let's see," I reminisced, "years ago the grocery stores bought oranges to sell and the fruit came packed in big wooden boxes which were called crates. They had a heavy wooden bottom and slats (I gestured with my hands), thinned sides of wood with space between. Best of all, there was a strong wooden divider in the middle to separate the fruit. People ate lots of oranges those days because there wasn't much choice of fruit shipped north in the wintertime. When the fruit was sold, the grocer would give the boxes to the people who asked for them. There were many uses for these wooden crates."

"We girls had five or six of these orange crates. We kept them in the attic. Attics were big rooms at the top of the house used to store things when they were not in use. On days we had to play indoors, we would carry the crates into the living room and play with them."

"Like what?" asked Tony.

"Sometimes we would line them in a row and pretend we had a train. People rode on trains from town to town in those days. Lots of store products came on the many trains which ran through our area. We would put our dolls, teddy bears and little kids in the crates and push them around making 'tooting' and 'whistling' sounds like a train. Mother said we scratched the linoleum and wore out the rug but she let us play train anyway. We took turns being Conductor saying, 'All Aboard!' and punching the paper train tickets which we made out of our tablet paper. This took time as we made the tickets and pretended to sell them to the passengers."

"Some days we played 'house' all day long. We set the crates on end and made cupboards and tables with them. The divider in the middle made a good shelf for dishes and pretend food. Mother had given us a piece of printed cloth, left from dressmaking. We gathered it on a string and tacked it on the crate to make a curtain for the cupboard. People sometimes made curtains for open shelves to make it look prettier in those days. We made paper doilies for the shelves and used a dish towel to cover the table crate. Many dolls and stuffed animals shared feasts with us. Our tea party food was usually soda or graham crackers, marshmallows and little cups of water, but we thought it tasted wonderful. One of the crates was our pretend stove. We used our crayolas to draw stove burners on the crate top. We pretended to cook our food on the crate stove. We used fruit jar covers, old pie pans and anything our mother had in the kitchen for kettles and plates. Our real china dishes were in the china cupboard and were too good to use for playing orange crate house."

"Tell me more about playing with crates!" Tony insisted.

"Sometimes we played Grocery Store," I explained. "This was a 'biggie.' We would beg cans and boxes from mother's kitchen. We made store shelves with the crates and put the food or stock on the shelves. One crate was laid flat and served as the store counter. We wrote on a homemade grocery sales pad. We wrote down the order or the list of items the customer wanted to buy. We took turns playing clerk and customer. For money we used big buttons and we also made dollars out of paper. This took time to make so we had plenty of things to do. We even had a toy telephone so we wrote down orders for groceries pretend people wanted to buy. Then we would take turns delivering these things."

"Peach canning season in the summertime was also fun as our mother canned many crates of peaches for our winter desserts. Peach crates were small and flat. The sides were about six inches high. They were made of wood but were not as strong as orange crates. We could sit in them and stretch our legs out. Since these crates were in plentiful supply, we could take them apart and use the wood to build marvelous things. We salvaged the nails and borrowed the kitchen hammer (not big enough to hurt us) and pounded away the hours building our secret projects."

"My sister always built an airplane out of peach crates. She made a propeller out of thin wood and nailed it to the front of the crate. She sat in her home-made airplane for hours and traveled around the world in her imagination."

"Peaches were canned in August so kids could play with the crates outside. Mother was happy as it kept her kitchen clear of children while she worked with hot jars of fruit."

"The ends of peach crates were used as markers for home plate and bases for our three member ball team or more if friends came to play."

Uses for these crates never ended. When we were finished playing with them, they were broken up as the wood made great kindling in the wood cooking stove."

Tony listened with utter fascination. He picked up his new Transformer and began making it into a space-age creature. He thought awhile and then lamented, "You sure were lucky to have crates to play with."

The Valentine Prize

The students of West Fork School and their teacher, Mary Wilson, had made elaborate plans to celebrate Valentine's Day. The year was 1945 and World War II was dragging on. The students of West Fork, ready for some enjoyment and relief from the sameness of wintertime, looked forward to the February 14th Valentine Party. A large Valentine box had been lovingly decorated by the twenty-eight students of this one-room rural school. Homemade Valentines had been put into the box, one by one. Some pupils purchased Valentines for their "secret" boy or girl friend, special friends and Miss Wilson.

The snow was deep outside and the wind was blowing but it was cheerful and warm inside the school house. The pot-bellied stove was rosey red, black paper silhouettes of Presidents Lincoln and Washington hung on the north wall as a sign of patriotism, part of the February birthday celebration for these revered presidents. Valentine hearts and lace doilies in every window brightened the classroom.

Party day arrived. After the last recess, the wet mittens and scarves were hung near the stove to dry. Snowy boots were shoved into the cloak room with the dinner pails and the students were in a party mood.

The Valentine committee had decided each person would tell a story or poem for entertainment. Miss Wilson had promised to tell a story from her childhood. Since they had all studied hard since Christmas vacation and behaved well, she also promised a very special surprise treat on Valentine's Day. She told them, "I don't even know what the treat will be." This was an intriguing puzzle. Why didn't the teacher know?

The fun began. Miss Wilson played the piano and they all sang, "I Love You Truly," "Let Me Call You Sweetheart," "Row, Row, Row Your Boat." The younger children could follow most of the words in the "Golden Book of Songs."

Names were then drawn, one at a time, from a stocking cap, to determine whose turn to tell a story or recite a poem.

Several of the first and second graders recited:

> "Roses are red,
> Violets are blue,
> Sugar is sweet
> And so are you."

A few of the younger children had older brothers and sisters to help and they came up with such rhymes as:

> "I love you little,
> I love you big,
> I love you like
> A little pig."

After every recitation everybody clapped.

As older pupils took their turns they told little secrets. Mavis, seventh grade, told of getting a letter from a boy she met during the summer vacation.

Andy told about the 4-H calf that won a purple ribbon at the County Fair (a story everybody had heard a dozen times) but they clapped anyway.

Joe, grade eight, who was always cutting-up, told an involved story about an ugly boy he met in town and thought Marie should send him a Valentine.

Marie sort of had a "case" on Joe so she didn't know if she liked the story or not. She shyly said she admired one of the students. She refused to give his name, but everybody knew.

After each had taken a turn, it was time for Miss Wilson to share her story. This would be a biggie, they hoped.

Miss Wilson revealed her story:

"I grew up in a small town and the neighbor boy was just my age. His name was David and we played together almost every day because there were no other children our age in the area. I liked to play the boys' games and he liked reading books, playing house and coloring at my house. We walked to school together every day. One day we each had a box of crackerjack. We opened them and each had a prize. Mine was a little red rubber ball and I gave it to David. His box had a ring with a red set. It was beautiful, I thought. He gave it to me and secretly whispered that it was because he loved me and that we might get married someday.

I wore the ring everyday. I was in second grade and we were playing in the snow at recess. I took off my mitten and before I realized it, my ring was gone. I ran into the school crying, "I lost my diamond!" I told my teacher. She said, "What did it look like?" I cried, "It was a *red* one!" I cried so hard that my teacher asked everyone to look for it but we couldn't find it. That night, when we walked home from school, David told me, "Someday I'll get you another ring."

David moved, with his family, to another city. I didn't see him again until this summer when he came to visit me. He is now in the U.S. Navy and is on a ship in the South Pacific Ocean. We write letters back and forth almost every day. I told him about school and the Valentine Party we were planning. His ship was docked in Hawaii last month and he sent a package for us. He wrote that we should open it at this party. I don't have any idea what is in the package."

By this time, the pupils were bug-eyed with the story and anticipated surprise. Miss Wilson pulled out a cardboard box from the storage closet. It was plastered with stamps and addressed to "Miss Mary Wilson." It had a Hawaiian postmark. The students left their desks and crowded around the package. Miss Wilson used her scissors to cut open the tape. As she opened the box she found fancy sea shells, wrapped in papers, one for each student. There was a small box, wrapped in pink paper, and labeled, "THE TEACHER." Miss Wilson passed the package for each child to choose a sea shell. Then, she carefully unwrapped the paper from her gift and stood looking at it. It was a box of crackerjack but it did not look sealed on the end. Miss Wilson just stared at it. Marie suggested she open the box to see what was inside. In chorus everybody yelled, "Open it!"

She pulled out a small white box which had a note glued to it. She peeked in the box and screamed, "Oh my goodness!" In her excitement she read the note aloud, "I told you I'd give you another ring sometime. When this darn war is over you can set a wedding date. Love, David."

The room was in turmoil with everyone shouting and laughing. Miss Wilson sat weakly in her chair. Finally, she slipped the ring on her finger and held it out for all to see.

The party progressed. The big Valentine box was opened and all the little love hearts and messages were distributed, Miss Wilson served red Kool-aid in paper cups and put a small chocolate heart on each desk.

The clock neared four o'clock; time to dismiss. Tomorrow would be Saturday! Life was good in West Fork School even though a war was being fought around the world and Miss Wilson's boyfriend, David, was on a ship in the Pacific Ocean.

The happy kids gathered up their clothes, packed their books, Valentines, sea shells and candy in their lunch pails and pockets and left the building laughing and shouting.

Miss Wilson sat at her desk, staring at the beautiful diamond. She read the note again. Tears rolled down her cheeks but she grabbed her little desk calendar and tried to figure out a good time to have a wedding.

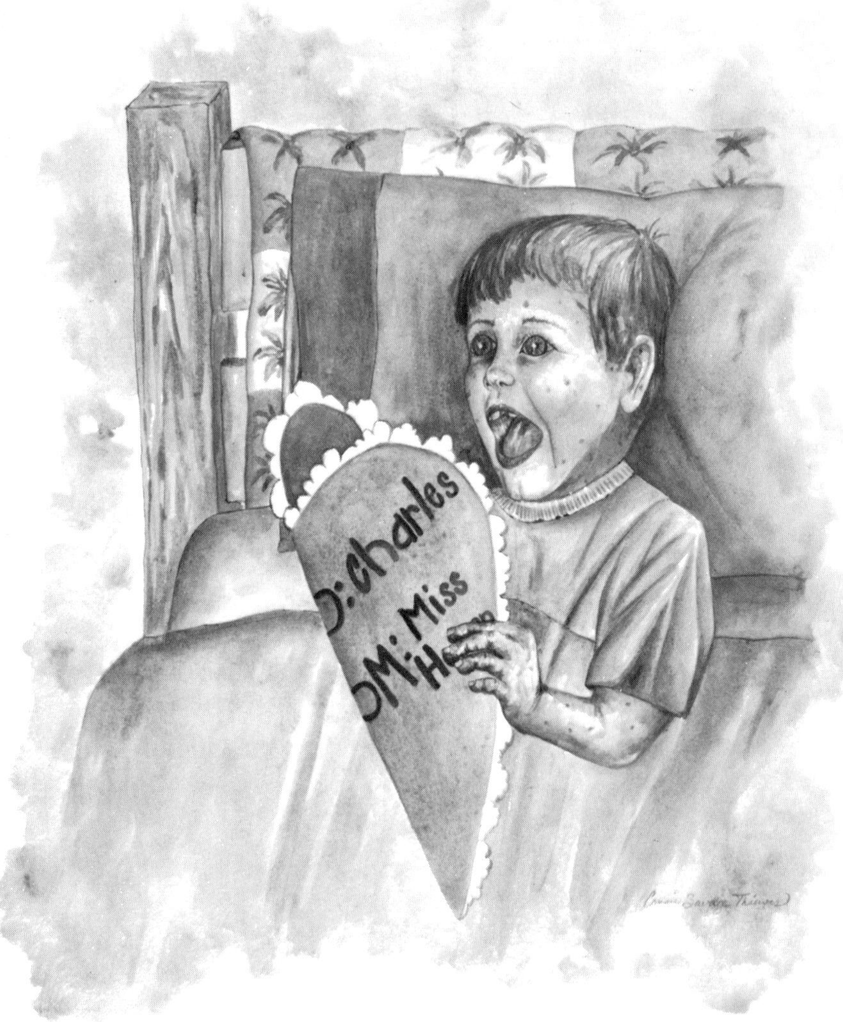
charles
Miss

The Cupid's Arrow

Charles Dahlmeyer was the only second grader in Clearfield Rural School and he loved it. The new teacher was Miss June Hansen. She was nineteen years old and had attended the Normal Training School the previous year to obtain her teaching certificate. Clearfield was her first school and she loved it.

There were 35 students in the one room school but only students in six of the grades. This made an easier schedule than teaching all eight grades. Miss Hansen had attended a country school herself so she knew how to juggle the time and classes to teach the important "South Dakota Course of Study" outlined by the State Department of Education and supervised by the County Superintendent of Schools.

Miss Hansen's job was not an easy one but the students helped with the janitorial chores and she was fortunate to know the families in her district. She lived in one of their homes and rode to school with the children.

Since Charlie was the only second grader, Miss Hansen spent time helping him with his numbers and phonics. He could do his own work unless the lessons being taught to the older children became too interesting and then he would pause to listen. Miss Hansen was patient in helping him sound out the reading words. Her voice was soft and she smelled of the Apple Blossom Cologne his big sisters used so sparingly ... or was it "Evening in Paris"? he mused. At any rate, Charlie had liked Miss Hansen from the first day of school and by Christmas time he decided that maybe he was "in love" with her. At least, he often heard his big sisters talking about "in love" and this must be what it was like.

School was almost fun. The best part was the art class which was held the last hour of school on Fridays. After Christmas vacation the art class project was to make paper snowflakes. This was fun. Even the little kids could fold the squares and circles of white paper many times, then cut out little curlicues and designs. Open the paper and a filigree of lace looked like a snowflake. Miss Hansen said, "No two snowflakes are alike." Neither were these. The students hung these masterpieces in all the windows, which were on the south side of the room. The light or sun shining through these paper designs helped to brighten the many drab days of January.

At the end of January, the snowflakes came down and the older children made silhouettes of Presidents Lincoln and Washington. They were made of black paper and looked like the pictures of the two great presidents whose pictures hung on either side of the blackboard. Charlie had listened to the sixth and seventh grade history classes which exemplified these patriotic men. He eavesdropped on these stories until he almost forgot to do his numbers. When the black likenesses of the presidents hung in the windows Charlie decided they were the most important men in the world.

During the first art class in February, Miss Hansen told the students about plans for a school Valentine Party. "The party," she said, "will be at 3 o'clock on Friday, the 13th of February." The year was 1935. He heard some of the girls talk at recess and they said, "Friday the 13th can be an unlucky day." But nobody really believed it.

During art class the students made Valentines and they could work on them during free time. They made folded notes and wrote sentimental verses in them. They let their imaginations run wild as to decoration. Some even made envelopes out of manila paper. The room smelled like the white library paste they used. The older girls made a large Valentine box as a receptacle for these love messages. They decorated the box with hearts and flowers. There was a big white cupid, with an arrow, on the top. The girls said the cupid meant "love" but Charlie wasn't sure of the connection between this naked child, with wings and an arrow, and love.

The day before the party the students finished their projects. Charlie had an idea and he proceeded to make the Valentine of his heart's desire. It was his secret Valentine. He cut a big red heart from school construction paper. He covered the back with paste and centered it on a lace paper doily. With his black crayola he printed "Miss June Hansen" just like it was chalked on the blackboard. In the very smallest of letters, he printed his name on the back. As a final touch, he printed a large LOVE in the center of the heart.

When the students had their heads in a book or were doing their written work, Charlie slipped to the back of the room, with the pretense of getting a drink from the water pail, and he quickly slipped the love message into the big box. His heart was pounding when he returned to his desk. His face felt flushed. After a few minutes he realized he really was thirsty, so he went back for another drink. Actually, he didn't feel very well. He hoped that this wasn't the "love sick" he had heard about.

After school he walked home with his sisters, while his older brothers ran ahead. He didn't feel like running. The cold air felt good on his face but his eyes felt scratchy. He decided he was just excited about the big party tomorrow.

Friday morning Charlie knew he was sick. He itched all over and there were little bumps on his chest. He called to his mother, who came into the bedroom and asked Charlie why he wasn't dressed for school. Then she looked at him and exclaimed, "Charlie, you have the chicken pox!"

Charlie's mother knew and Charlie knew going to school was out of the question. Charlie began to cry. He didn't want to miss the Valentine Party. He knew he was too big to cry but he was heart-broken. By this time, his sisters and brothers had gathered to find out why Charlie wasn't coming to the breakfast table. They all sympathized with him and promised to bring home his Valentines and even the heart-shaped cookie they would have for a treat. Charlie was not consoled. He wailed, "You can bring home my Valentines but you can't bring home all the FUN!"

The sick boy spent the day in bed feeling lousy both inside and outside. He stayed in bed because he was too miserable to do anything else. He was dozing when the kids came home from school. They were laughing and talking about the great party. Charlie hid under the covers. Then his sister pulled the quilt back and handed him a large manila envelope. Charlie looked inside and pulled out a giant red paper heart with lace all around. It was beautiful. Miss Hansen had printed, in black ink, "We miss you, Charlie. Get well soon! Love. Miss Hansen."

The surprise was too much for Charlie and a tear ran down his nose and dripped off the end. Miss

Hansen loved him, too! The arrow's sting had left his heart. The kids had brought "some of the fun" home to him. Maybe Friday, the 13th, wasn't the unluckiest day in the world.

A Birthday Surprise

Agnes and John Meyer were married in 1932. They moved to a make-shift three-room home on a ranch in central South Dakota. The ranch was located across the section from John's parents. The plan was to make improvements to the young couple's ranch as soon as possible. The house had been built at the turn-of-the-century and left much to be desired. Many of the pioneer sod homes had better insulation and afforded more protection from the cold winds of the prairies. The dilapidated barn on the ranch had been repaired first to make sure the animals were protected in a decent building. The old motto of farmer and rancher was, "The barn can build the house, but the house can't build the barn." First, the outbuildings were repaired and if there was money left the house was repaired.

By 1934 the couple and their new baby were still living in the house which lacked any conveniences except a cistern pump in a lean-to shed on the side of the house. There was a kitchen equipped with a black, cast-iron Southern Comfort cookstove. This took wood and cobs like a hungry monster to keep the kitchen warm enough to separate milk, cook meals and use as a washroom. The main room, used for "living" was connected between the kitchen and an added-on shed-like room called the bedroom. A wooden rod across the end of the bedroom served as a closet. A chrome and black, cast-iron Heatrola stove stood in the living room. It was square in shape and had isinglass windows to allow the heat to escape. This stove burned hard coal but had to be kindled with cobs, wood and paper if the fire went out. It also had to be "banked" at night to insure a morning fire. Keeping the stoves going, including removal of ashes, was an almost full-time job for the woman of the house if she wanted to keep warm during the "depth of a South Dakota winter."

By early March, John was complaining to Agnes about the amount of fuel they had used to keep the stoves going.

"You know, Agnes," he declared one bitter-cold morning, "if this cold weather continues we'll have to cut more wood. I'll bet the folk's wood pile is about gone, too."

That very afternoon John's father, Mike, rode his horse to the ranch from across the pastures. He came into the kitchen, downed a cup of coffee from the pot on the cookstove and announced, "John, we're about out of fuel over there! You and I are going to have to spend a day or two cutting trees. The wood won't be cured but we need it. There are some dead poplars standing on the north quarter so we could cut those."

John shook his head as he gulped some coffee and responded, "Gosh, I hate to go wood-cutting in this cold weather but we don't have a choice."

"How about tomorrow?" his dad suggested. "Should we get back from the cutting late you can stay with us if Agnes can handle the baby and things here." John agreed. Agnes was almost sick with the thought of a night alone and all the chores around the ranch. She would dearly have loved to take baby Anna and spend the day with her mother-in-law. She knew her husband's mother was thinking how much she'd like the company but her situation was the same. "If I don't stay home, the fires will go out and everything in the house will freeze solid in this weather," she thought.

After his father left, John said, "I sure wish you could spend the day with mother but we have to cut wood as late as possible tomorrow evening. The evening chores will have to be done here and the chickens fed ... then there is the milking ... and the fires. You and Anna can spend a day with mother as soon as this weather lets up."

Next morning John did the chores, brought in an extra bucket of coal and a bushel basket of cobs. He then hitched the team of horses to the lumber wagon loaded with the ladder and a bucksaw. He stopped by the house again. He kissed Agnes goodbye and admonished, "Now don't you worry none about me! I'll be alright and I'll bring you a load of wood. Be sure to give the cows plenty of hay. Don't expect me home until about noon tomorrow." Then he was off down the road in the swirling snow.

After John left, Agnes took hot water from the cookstove reservoir and washed the breakfast dishes. She bathed, changed and fed little Anna and then rocked and played with her in the south kitchen window. When Anna fell asleep for her morning nap Agnes went to the barn to check the cattle and gather eggs ... there were two large eggs. The hens weren't laying well this time of year.

Upon her return, she shoveled the ashes out of the stove, swept the floors and added more coal to the living room heater. She then placed the two eggs, carefully, into the speckled bowl on the shelf and counted them. She had ten eggs. She had been hoarding the eggs for a surprise birthday cake for John who would be thirty years old on Friday. She hoped to get two more eggs in the morning as the cake took twelve egg whites. Her plan was to make John's favorite cake, angel food.

Agnes took down her recipe notebook and found her mother's recipe for "Prize Angel Food." She read it carefully.

PRIZE ANGEL FOOD CAKE

12 egg whites   1 cup sifted cake flour
1½ cups granulated sugar
½ tsp. salt
1¼ tsp. cream of tartar
1 tsp. double-strength vanilla

Method:

    Separate eggs and place whites in large mixing bowl. (Save yolks for cookies or salad dressing.)
    Sift cake flour and sugar before measuring.
    Sift the 1 cup cake flour, salt and ½ cup sugar together in flour sifter ten times. Sift onto waxed paper.
    Whip egg whites with wire whip until foamy, sprinkle cream of tartar over top; continue to whip until egg whites are stiff and hold soft peaks, do not whip dry.
    Gradually whip in, one teaspoon at a time, one cup of sugar; whip well after each addition. Then use a large spoon to carefully fold in flour-sugar mixture a little at a time. Blend in vanilla.
    Pour mixture into an ungreased angel food (tube) pan. Run a knife through batter in widening circles to break air bubbles.
    Bake cake in moderate oven at 375° for 15 minutes. Reduce heat to 250° and bake 50 minutes. Do not peek for first 40 minutes. Remove cake from oven and turn upside down with middle of cake on a bottle or funnel until cake is cool. If pan does not have "legs," cake may be turned over three cups for support.

Agnes was puzzled about the temperature. Her old wood/cob stove had a temperature gauge on the front but it was hard to regulate the right heat. However, her mother had put a note at the bottom of the recipe.

"Grandma said to let the cob fire in the stove die down to red (no flame) before putting the cake in the oven, watch carefully, and then add 3 or 4 cobs (depending upon their size) to the fire every fifteen minutes. After 45 minutes use a clean broom straw to test the doneness. If straw comes out clean, cake is done."

Agnes had made an angel food cake before she was married, under her mother's supervision. It turned out well so she was confident she could do it now if the hens cooperated with two more eggs in the morning. She would have a great surprise for John's birthday. Surely the hens would lay two more eggs in the morning and she could make the cake before John returned home at noon. John had been so busy with winter chores and the worry about wood-cutting that she was sure he had forgotten his birthday. All day she envisioned the beautiful cake.

By evening a major storm was brewing and the wind was whipping around the house. She kept the stoves going at a warmer-than-usual temperature since she hoped that conserving fuel was no longer a problem. After breaking the ice in the water tank for the cattle to drink, milking and feeding the cows and chickens, she brought old Sarge, the dog, inside the house and settled down with Anna beside the living room heater. Agnes gave Anna a bottle of milk. Agnes nibbled a sandwich.

Agnes lit the lamp early as the dark clouds outside made it darker than usual. She and Anna played peek-a-boo and little laughing games. Then she put the baby in the basket near the stove and began knitting John a birthday scarf by the light of the kerosene lamp. As she knit, she began to worry about the potatoes freezing. This had been a worry all winter so the couple had been in the habit of putting a sack of potatoes, which had been brought up from the cellar dug-out, under the covers at the foot of their bed. This way they were not too warm, as by the stove, and not in danger of freezing if the stove went out. As the windows fogged up and froze she also began to worry about the eggs. If she left them in the kitchen or living room and the heat was too low they would freeze... then no cake... no surprise.

After giving the problem serious thought she decided to put the eggs in a small box and put them in the bed beside her under the covers. That would make sure they wouldn't freeze. She sadly remembered how her houseplants had frozen one November night when an early storm surprised them. She couldn't take a chance with the birthday eggs.

The evening seemed very long and quiet except for the whistling wind, crackling fire and snoring of old Sarge. Little Anna was covered with a woolen quilt and was sleeping soundly in her bassinet. Agnes decided to go to bed early. She carefully banked the fire in the kitchen range and the coal heater. Before retiring she put the sack of potatoes at the foot of the bed and covered it with a rag rug from the bedroom floor. Next she moved Anna's bassinet close to her side of the bed and put the box of eggs under the covers where John usually slept. By nine o'clock she was sound asleep. Old Sarge would bark if anything unusual happened.

John and his father had decided to quit woodcutting early when the storm began to move in. They could finish the first decent day that came along. John thought maybe Agnes couldn't handle the chores with little Anna and the extra fuel needed to keep the house warm. After unloading some of the logs, helping his dad with the chores and eating supper with his parents, John left for his own ranch.

John noticed the lamp was not lit so he assumed Agnes was in bed. He unhitched the horses and tended to a few chores in the barn. The kerosene lantern in the barn was handy on a windy night since the wind could not blow it out. He let himself in the back door very quietly and undressed behind the glowing coals of the heater. Sarge hardly moved.

He peeked under the blanket to view his tiny, sleeping daughter and then let his weary body sink into the mattress in bed. Immediately he heard, "crack-crunch-crack!" He jumped out of bed; simultaneously Agnes gave out a yell and awoke little Anna who began to cry. John lit the dresser lamp and tried to explain to Anges, who was frantically pulling a crushed box out from under the bed clothes. "My eggs! My birthday eggs!" she cried.

Finally she fell in John's arms crying and laughing at the same time. He tried to comfort her. Baby Anna fell back to sleep and Agnes explained how she had planned a surprise cake for his birthday.

The two took the dripping box to the kitchen table where they sorted out cracked and broken eggs and rescued what they could. He was touched by her story of the surprise angel food cake and soothed her with, "Honey, you know I love scrambled eggs. You can fix me a batch for breakfast and I'd love a custard pie for my birthday."

The next morning the sun was shining and the hens surprised them with four eggs. Agnes made the scrambled egg breakfast and the custard pie, with nutmeg topping, served as a wonderful birthday treat for John.

The next year the REA came through electrifying the neighborhood. The Meyers families were the first to sign up. John also promised Agnes, "I'll build a better house as soon as the price of cattle goes up!"

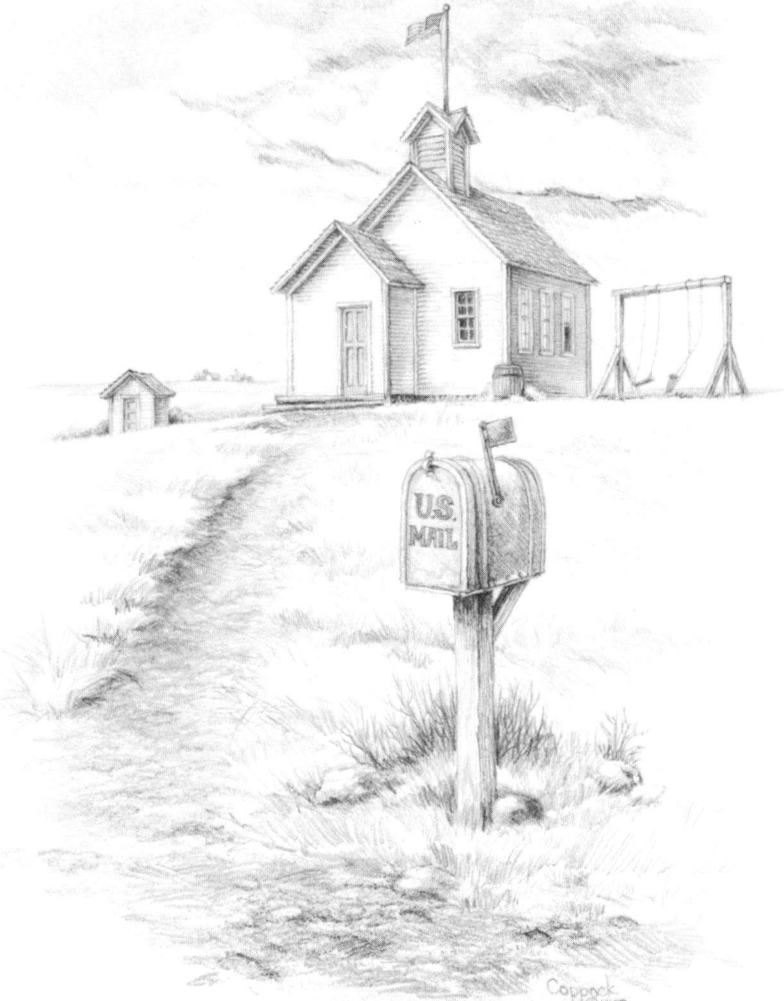
U.S.
MAIL
Coppock
©1989

April Fool in Country School

The names and places have been changed to protect the guilty.

Today April Fool's Day comes and goes without ripple in the public school system. Most students don't know that tricks played on April 1st are in the category of "just foolin'—no hard feelings—just fun." Little recognition is given to the day which used to rank with Halloween, May Day and Valentine's Day for youthful fun.

In the days of rural country schools, April Fool's Day was looked forward to with great anticipation. It was a day for fun and a reprieve from an otherwise dull time of year. The day, April 1, was usually a blustery day. It was too cold to play outside and there was little new to stimulate interest inside at recess time or during noon hour. Rural school students were used to making their own fun as their facilities and equipment were sparse. Therefore, imagination played a large part in their fun time. All Fool's Day was one day that broke the monotony of sameness in the school day routine. It was a time for "silly" jokes and tricks. The teachers were happy when the day was past but they looked upon it as a time for a little wit and witticism.

Fifty years ago, the students at Prairie Lane Rural School were tired of winter. The March temperatures had been below normal, the building was drafty and the kids had coughs and sniffles. They were ready for spring. For a week or more the bright spot was thinking of harmless pranks to play on each other and Miss Torgelson, their teacher, on the Fool's Day.

The primary grade children weren't sure what to do for a trick but third and fourth graders had reviewed every potential prank of the past such as: a tack on the teacher's chair (Miss Torgelson was too nice for this nasty trick), gum on a chair (not much fun), announce that the County Superintendent's car was headed up the road (everyone would scramble to clean up the room and look studious – not fun, and done two years ago), "I see a hole in your sock!" (too common to cause alarm to the victim), and "The clock stopped!" (Miss Torgelson had gotten a watch for Christmas). One couldn't tell another he was wanted on the telephone as there wasn't a phone in the schoolhouse. Once a student had put salt in the drinking pail but everyone suffered and the teacher had to thaw out the hand pump to get more water. Tying coat sleeves together, hiding the chalk and saying a mouse was running in the room were worn out gags.

Leona Jones and Laura Meyer were both in eighth grade. They had been studying for the Achievement test, based on the State Course of Study, which would be given at the County Superintendent's office in May. They had to pass this test to graduate from eighth grade. They were tired of cramming for this test. The two had been racking their brains for a good joke to play on the Henderson girls, Alice, who was in seventh grade, and Edna, who was in sixth. They had been "stuck up" since Christmas vacation when they had visited an aunt in Sioux City. They had bragged about eating in a cafeteria and seeing a cinema. "The show featured Carol Lombard and

Robert Taylor," they said. Alice and Edna insinuated those who had not visited a big city were "Country Hicks" – the last thing any of them wanted to be – especially Leona and Laura. These eighth grade girls really wanted to play a good one on the Hendersons but nothing really good enough had come to mind.

April 1st rolled around and their bag of tricks was empty – no ideas! The day dawned unusually warm and beautiful. The two plotters arrived at school early and stayed outside the one room country school to think of something. Just then the mail man drove up to the mail box at the end of the lane and put something into the box. The two raced down to pick up the mail. To their surprise they found two small packages labeled "Box Holder." The packages were covered with a slip-on wrapper and inside each was a sample of laxative – X-Lax. They stood for a minute and thought. The idea they had been looking for came to their minds simultaneously! They would pretend to eat a candy bar, since the sample was enclosed in the same kind of foil as a Hershey bar. They would fix those Henderson girls!

When they came into the school room, Miss Torgelson asked if there were any letters in the box. They replied, "no letters." Miss Torgelson's attention drifted to other things.

During the morning Laura and Leona would hide their faces in their geography books and pretend to nibble from a candy bar. They made sure that one or both of the Henderson girls were watching. When recess came, Alice and Edna confronted them. The Henderson girls threatened to tell Miss Torgelson if Laura and Leona didn't share their candy. The pranksters claimed innocence at first. They then confessed but said they only had a little candy left but they would share if Edna and Alice didn't tattle. They promised and each girl gave a couple of small squares of the forbidden candy to one of the girls. The trick had worked! They could hardly keep straight faces. Originally they had planned to say "April Fool" but as soon as the Henderson girls ate the X-Lax they changed their minds and decided to let nature take its course.

Shortly after the noon lunch, first Alice and then Edna raised hands and asked permission to be excused. This meant putting on coats and boots and taking the path to the outhouse behind the schoolhouse. It was a trip made only out of necessity. Within a half hour, the girls made the same request. Miss Torgelson thought they must have eaten something which did not agree with them. After another "run" to the outhouse, the Henderson girls were happy to see four o'clock dismissal time roll around.

All afternoon Leona and Laura did not dare look at each other. They kept their heads buried in their studies. Miss Torgelson complimented them on their diligence.

Several days after Fool's Day, it was Leona's turn to start the fire in the school stove at 8 a.m. Laura offered to come early to help. The older students took turns starting the fire so it would be warm when school began. Actually many of the students knew more about fire-building than Miss Torgelson who had grown up in town with the luxury of a coal furnace. The girls shook down the ashes and built a new fire with paper, cobs and kindling. The two were still having their private chuckles over the prank they had played. A little coal was added to the instant flames. They waited and watched the fire as they visited.

The building was getting warm when the Henderson family arrived. Their father had brought them in the car, which was unusual since it was a warm day and they lived only a half mile from school and usually walked. To the amazement of Leona and Laura the Henderson girls were wearing dark, tinted glasses, called "sun glasses." "Maybe it was something they had learned in Soo City!" the older girls whispered snidely. Any novelty in rural school was worthy of exploring to the 'nth degree so they were curious.

The Henderson girls put their coats in the clock room, stashed their lunch buckets in the back closets (the coolest area in the school), and began looking at the library books at the back of the room. They then sat in their desks to do school work.

Leona and Laura had put more coal into the Heatrola stove and were whispering to each other. Finally, they couldn't stand it longer and Laura meekly asked, "Could we try on your glasses, please!" Without a comment, the girls were given the curiosity pieces. It was fun to try them on and look at the sun, stare at the snow, try to read the blackboard and look into the mirror over the wash dish. The girls pretended they were movie stars as they loked into the mirror. Finally their curiosity had diminished and they returned the glasses to the Henderson girls and went after another bucket of coal. As they fetched the coal, they remarked if the April Fool's joke had been known the Henderson girls would not have let them try on the glasses.

Several days later, Laura and Leona realized the Henderson girls' gesture of generosity in loaning them the dark spectacles was not one of pure unselfishness and endearment. Alice and Edna had figured out the April Fool "trick" when their mother had also received a "Box Holder" package of laxative in their mailbox.

But the pranksters were rewarded with a late April Fool's joke.

Laura and Leona caught a bad case of PINK EYE, too!

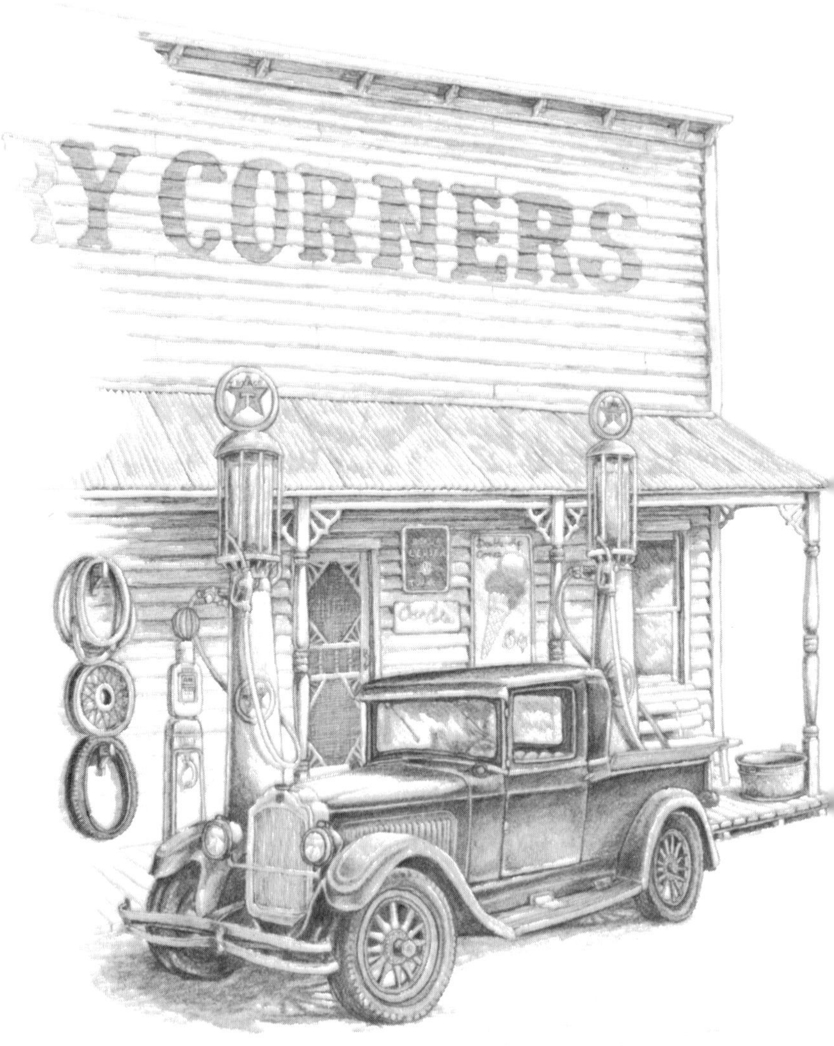
Y CORNERS

A Country Charivari

Dave's Family Barber Shop, complete with a red and white striped pole outside the door, was typical of the small town business of yesteryear. The shop was a mecca for exchange of news, farm prices and opinions, political views and gossip during the pre-electric razor day. Unshaven men took turns sitting in the row of chairs along the barbershop wall waiting to get to the head of the line and hear the word, "Next!" At that word, the man in the head chair would sit in the adjustable barber's chair, have a large white apron whipped around his body, a hot, damp towel placed over his face before being lathered with white, foamy soap. At this time, the man's conversation was halted as the barber carefully, with short, quick strokes, shaved cream and whiskers off the man's face. Once the face was pink and shaven the barber sprinkled a tonic into his palms, then deftly patted the elixir onto the man's cheeks. With a swish of a feathery brush, he fluffed talcum powder around the man's neck, whipped off the apron, collected the twenty-five cents, and the man was shaven and ready for a Saturday night date or Sunday morning church.

Between shaves the barber sharpened his straight-edge razor on a black leather strap which was fastened to the edge of the barber chair. "Next!" meant the man's turn at the ritual which continued until every farmer who wanted a "shave in town" was accommodated. The town men and merchants were expected to get their shaves earlier on Saturdays so the farmers could be shaven while their wives were buying groceries and their cream was being tested.

Snatches of conversation from the row of men waiting for a shave on a hot August night in 1938:

> Pete: "I hear the new school 'marm' for the Patterson School is sure a good looker."
> Jess: "Yup, I suppose she'll make her play for P. P. Patterson like the rest of them gals done."
> Johnnie: "No gal will catch him! He's got it too easy with his ma and dad right there to make life comfortable for him. Can't beat being an only child. He got to go to Ag College and he farms like they told 'em there."
> Pete: "Guess it paid off. Look at the crops he gets with them new methods, but I doubt if the guy will ever get married."
> Jess: "Naw, they don't call him "Pinch-Penny Patterson" for nothing..."
> Barber Dave: "Next."

Another customer enters the barber shop and the conversations speculate whether or not it will rain next week.

In truth P. P. Patterson was a pretty prosperous farmer. Being an only son and the grandson of homesteaders whose choice farm land lay adjacent to Willow Ridge, SD, with Spring Creek dissecting the west quarter, had advantages. Also, P.P. had the luxury of graduating from the South Dakota Agricultural College at Brookings. With his ROTC training, he served in the army during World War

II. He returned home with a rank of Major. His dream was realized in returning to the family farm and putting his college knowledge into practice. The neighbors called his methods "new-fangled" but most of them paid off very well.

Homer and Edith Patterson talked about retiring and moving into town but decided to stay on the farm as long as P. P. was single and needed them. Edith, known as one of the best cooks in her Extension Club, baked pies, cakes and all the goodies her son, Peter Patrick Patterson, enjoyed eating. In recent years, she hoped that one or another of the school teachers who taught the Patterson District III Rural School, located on the northeast corner of their section, would interest P. P. enough to marry and eventually give them some grandchildren. It seemed none of the teachers, and none of the local girls, were of interest to their son. They showed interest in him but he paid little or no attention to their overtures.

Edith and Homer had a glimmer of hope during the 1946-47 school term as P. P. suddenly took an interest in the happenings at the Patterson School. He would visit the school and teacher Miss Mary Ann Hunter to inquire if there was an adequate coal supply for the furnace. He fixed the broken swing on the playground and shoveled the snow from the front steps in December. After the Christmas program, he helped remove the wires strung through sheets which were curtains for the stage area. He stayed after they left the school program and when he came home he was whistling.

The conversation in Dave's Family Barber Shop in the spring of 1947 confirmed people's suspicions:

Peter: "I hear P. P. is taking quite an interest in the school these days!"

Jess: "Yup, he fixed the mail box when the snow plow knocked it down!"

Johnnie: "I heard that he took Miss Hunter to a movie in Sioux Falls last Sunday night. Anyway, my daughter, Katherine, told us that Miss Hunter had seen a show called, "The Bells of St. Mary" with Bing Crosby and Ingrid Bergman. When the kids asked her who took her she just sort of blushed and wouldn't say."

Peter: "You don't think P. P. would actually get married!"

Barber Dave: "Next!"

The news that P. P. Patterson and Miss Hunter were seeing each other soon trickled into the conversation of the women who met at Extension Club. From there, the news was discussed from woman to woman over the 15-party rural telephone line. In fact, there might as well have been a 'general ring' (when the operator rings a series of 'long' and 'short' rings until each receiver is picked up for an important message—such as: "There are cows in the road at the Olson's farm. Who do they belong to?" "Jones' barn is on fire. He needs help!" or "There were chicken thieves at Johnson's last night. Be on the look out in case they strike again!")

On Easter Sunday P. P. Patterson and Miss Mary Ann Hunter attended the early church service at the First Congregational Church and created such interest that the women forgot to pay attention to each other's hats and other accessories—gloves, scarves, and purses in fashion at the time.

On Monday morning, the women of the area finished hanging out their clothes and began their phone conversations:

> Emma: "I hear P. P. and Miss Hunter were in church together Sunday. Did you hear what she wore?"
>
> Marie: " I talked to Clara this morning and she said Miss Hunter wore a pink flowered dress and big-brimmed pink picture hat. Her gloves and purse were white and she had spectator pumps with a light tan trim. She really looked beautiful!"
>
> Operator: "I'm sorry to interrupt, but would you ladies hang up because Mr. Johnson needs the line to call the veterinarian."

Women hung up . . . picked up the receiver again in a few minutes to find out what Mr. Johnson's trouble might be.

By June first, school was out and the news was out! P. P. Patterson and Miss Hunter were engaged. People termed her diamond ring "a good-sized rock." Edith and Homer were looking at houses to buy in town. Homer told everyone in the barber shop on Saturday night that they'd decided to retire.

The couple was married in Sioux Falls on June 29th, 1947 and they headed for the Black Hills on a honeymoon, according to what little news anyone could find out from Edith and Homer. This bit of news was the perfect reason for a celebration – a homecoming Charivari!

The conversation at Dave's Barber Shop on Saturday night concerned more the Charivari than Fourth of July.

> Jim: "I hear P. P. and Miss Hunter tied the knot and are honeymoonin' in the Hills."
> Pete: "We should have a Charivari when they come home."
> Johnnie: "Great idea, but when can we have it with haying and all?"
> Jess: "We'll find time! We'll make P. P. treat all of us. He should he happy enough since he married such a good looking gal."
> Barber Dave: "Next!"

As soon as the women and children heard the word "Charivari," their excitement mounted. The country telephone line buzzed with the news:

> Emma: "Pete says as soon as we know the newlyweds are home we'll have the Charivari. We can meet at our place and use our new hayrack for the party."
> Marie: "Haying or not, we'll be there!"
> Clara: "We'll make plans and then go the first night they are home as they won't expect it that soon. Johnnie says we'll take the bride and groom down main street in our new wheelbarrow."

The kids were squealing in the background and making plans for noisemakers.

On Wednesday afternoon, there was a general telephone ring. Every receiver was picked up to hear the important news.

The operator announced: "I've been asked to tell you that the John Olsons were in Chamberlain this morning and saw P. P. and Mary Ann eating at Al's Oasis. They said they had stopped at Wall Drug and they were going to visit cousins in Reliance and then plan to be home about chore-time tonight. The Charivariers are to meet at Thompson's place about nine o'clock tonight!"

The excitement accelerated. Women cooked early suppers. Men washed and changed into new overalls. Kids found every available noisemaker. They'd sure surprise the newlyweds!

By nine o'clock the cows had been milked and a caravan of assorted horse-drawn wagons and a few cars crept slowly down the road toward the Patterson farm. Lights were dimmed and as little noise as possible emitted from the group. Kids whispered to each other from corners of the hayrack.

Major Patterson had not served as an Army officer for nothing. He smelled a conspiracy which meant they could be subject to pranks of a Charivari. What he and his bride did not expect was the timing.

Pat and Mary Ann were in a mess that first night home from their honeymoon. They had the disks from their DeLaVal cream separator spread over the kitchen table trying to wash, wipe and reassemble the machine in a right order; a task Pat's mother performed routinely. The monster machine, used to separate the milk from the cream, took up space in the pantry so it would be warm. If the inside pieces were not washed after each use, the cream would taste sour. It was not a fun job.

In the midst of their confusion, the dogs perked up their ears and began to growl. The couple peered out their kitchen window and saw the procession coming up their driveway. "Charivariers!" they exclaimed simultaneously.

By then the crowd was at their back door and the couple went out to greet them. As soon as the clatter of washtubs pounded with aluminum water dippers, pails hit with sticks and soup ladles and the hand ringing of cowbells died down, the group assembled around the honeymooners. Shouting and yelling of "Surprise!" "Happy Marriage!" and "Treat or Tricks!" plus assorted good wishes greeted them.

Pat took control and announced, "Hey gang, we appreciate this but we just got home this noon and don't have a cookie or cracker in the house say nothing about drinks. If you forget about the wheelbarrow ride, we'll treat at Conner's Corner as soon as we can get there." A shout of approval went up from his friends and neighbors.

"Get the rest of your families and friends . . . kids too! We'll have a party!" he said.

The crowd hastily took their teams home, gathered up their hired men, younger children and grandparents who had been babysitting. The message of the Charivari party was passed around the neighborhood via another "general ring" on the party telephone line.

Pat quickly went to the telephone to call his friend and classmate, Tommy Conners, who operated Conner's Country Corner. This was a combination gas station, garage, short-order cafe and tavern. He told Tommy about the Charivari and to prepare for a crowd. He added, "Keep the tab of bills and I'll pay you next week . . . as soon as I sell the oats. Put some sawdust on the dance area, too 'cause some will want to dance."

Conners responded, "Great! We'll get ready."

The party was a huge success. P. P. kept feeding dimes into the juke box all evening playing the favorite tunes requested. The younger people danced and some of the older ones played cards in the cafe booths. The kids played outside until the mosquitoes got too bad and then came in to watch the action. At 11 p.m., Tommy Conners and his wife cooked hamburgers and hot dogs for everyone. Pop and beer was consumed in quantity and the kids got extra candy bars. Some of the kids brought nickels to buy gum.

The next week P. P. sold some grain and paid the bill at Conner's Corner with a smile. People talked about the Charivari all summer and told the tale to visiting friends and relatives. P. P. was now called Pat by his neighbors. Mrs. Mary Ann Patterson taught the Patterson Rural School until 1965 when the district was consolidated and the pupils were bused to Willow Ridge Consolidated School. Pat Patterson was elected president of the school board.

For years the housewives were reminded of the Charivari when they used their round-bottomed washtubs which had been pounded with the aluminum water dippers and never had a decent shape after that. Most of the cowbells were lost in the excitement of the event. But the memory was permanent.

Grandchildren and great-grandchildren have now heard about the big Charivari held for the newlyweds nearly fifty years ago. After hearing Grandpa tell the tale at a cousin's wedding, little Gregory asked his father, "Why can't we have a Charivari and get all that free candy and pop?" The affair sounded like a royal ball to him.

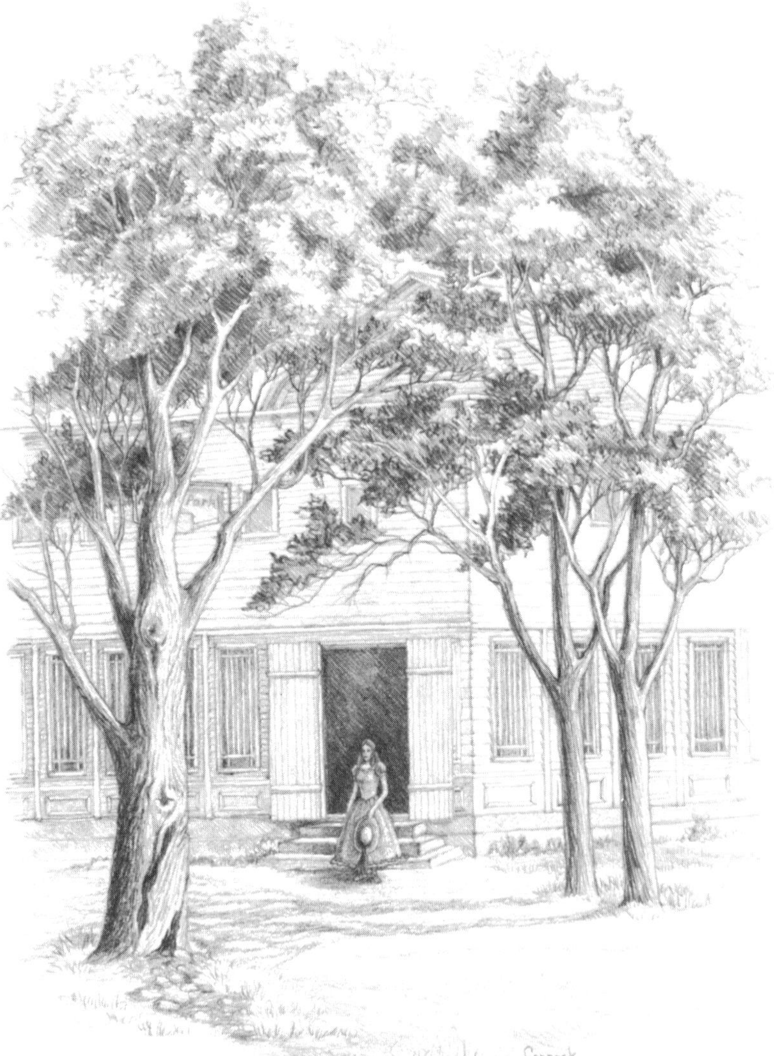
Coppock

A Gone With the Wind Romance

Sylvia Fischer had been drooling over the 1940 Spring and Summer Wish Book since it arrived in the mail on a snowy March day. The wish book was everyone's term for a mail-order catalog. The cover was frayed and the pages dog-eared as Sylvia spent leisure time wishing for clothes to fulfill her dreams.

The 16-year-old midwest farm girl had read the current best-selling novel "Gone With the Wind," by Margaret Mitchell, during the previous winter. She wished to emulate the main character, Scarlett O'Hara. Several months later she saw the premier movie based on the book and her desires were ignited to become an actress. The show's leading lady, Vivien Leigh, and hero, Clark Gable, were her cinematic idols. She decided wearing glamorous clothes was the first step to fulfilling her hoped-for career and meeting a handsome Hollywood hero.

The new catalog featured two items of clothing for which she yearned. They could further her present goals. Page 395 showed a "Gone With the Wind" dress and page 402 pictured a wide-brimmed Leghorn straw hat. If she could buy this outfit and wear it in the July 4th celebration, it could be the start of an exciting future.

The desired dress was described as: "An elegant, regale gown with bodice front, fastened with pearl buttons; the skirt designed in full-flare of five yards around the hemline; 100 percent cotton paisley print;

choice: cardinal red or navy blue; price: $6.99." The model was sitting on a grassy hillside with the skirt spread full-circle around her. Her face was shaded by a large hat.

The hat of her dreams was described as: "An enticing, tantalizing bonnet of glistening Leghorn straw; a three-inch sweeping brim with a provocative allure; choice of color: luggage tan or sky blue; price: $2.99."

Sylvia's mother was unimpressed. She said, "The skirt is cotton and will shrink and fade. The hat is too impractical and too 'adult' for you!" Sylvia was not convinced. "It's guaranteed!" she retorted. She was sure the outfit would guarantee a great time at the picnic. At least an ardent admirer might be found, although the advertisement did not state who might be "enticed or tantalized" by the attire.

Unheeded by her mother's advice, she hoarded nickels and pennies, her birthday money and allowance until she had ten dollars for the clothing and $1.25 postage needed to bring the outfit to her rural mail box. In ordering the clothing, it had been a tough decision as to colors. She settled on the cardinal red dress and sky blue hat. She decided that the luggage tan would not set off her auburn hair to full advantage.

Fresh in her mind was her embarrassment at last year's picnic when she had to wear a cotton striped dress Aunt Emma had made for her. "I felt like Bo-Peep," she said to herself, remembering the lack of boys looking her way when she was fifteen. "This year will be different," she promised herself. "I want a good-looking boy to skate WITH me," she declared as she pressed her ear close to the radio, listening to the WNAX Bohemian Band play a polka.

The mailman delivered the package the last week of June, just when she had begun to worry it might not arrive in time. She tried the dress on . . . it fit... sort of! The hat was big but a little brown rubber band was provided to adjust the size. "Maybe I should borrow some of mother's hat pins," she thought. "Well, I'll wear orange lipstick. I saw some Tangee at the dime store so they will have new shades of lipstick."

The Fischer's July 4th celebration was always spent at Ruskin Park, located about 15 miles from their farm. It was an annual event and their neighbors and friends would all be there. The park was located along the scenic James River with large cottonwood trees providing shade. A large pavilion was used for roller skating and dancing. Lawrence Welk and other popular bands played for dances. The Six Fat Dutchmen, another popular dance group, packed a crowd at Ruskin Park. A race track provided auto racing to delight the people who enjoyed watching the sport. Ball games, horseshoe, roller skating, dancing and the big fireworks display at dusk was enough excitement for all ages. Everyone in the area gathered there to commemorate the day.

This year the Fischers had a problem. Two days before the celebration their hired man quit to take other work. A new man would not come until after the 4th. There was no one to do the evening chores: milk cows, pick eggs, feed and water pigs and cattle, shut the chickens in the coop and brake the windmill if it got windy. Sylvia lamented, "I'll just DIE if I can't go!"

The following morning an unexpected solution arrived. Walter Johnson, the 17-year-old neighbor boy, rode his horse to the Fischer's to borrow a hack-saw for his father and deliver a recipe wanted by Mrs. Fischer. "Walt is a good kid," Sylvia's father often remarked. High school friends teased Walt about being sweet on Sylvia, who was lukewarm to Walt's interests. She had gone to ball games with him, but he was almost like a brother to her. The Fischer's sons, Timmy and Thomas, Jr., were in grade school so Walter was Sylvia's friend and handy companion. Her ideas of a wished-for boyfriend were gleaned from "Screen Play," "Movieland" and "True Confessions" magazines her mother didn't know she had under her mattress. Her aspirations of becoming an actress did not include Walter. The picnic problem caused her to declare, "I'll never marry a farmer or rancher! They always have to do chores! There is no glamour in farming!"

Sylvia was washing the separator when Walt came to the back door. Her mother invited him in for a glass of lemonade and a cookie. Sylvia kept working without looking up. When Walt asked about their July 4th plans Sylvia blurted, "We have to stay home. There is no one to do the chores." Walter sipped his lemonade and munched a cookie while he listened to Mrs. Fischer's explanation. He sized up the situation and suggested, "I'll do your chores...love to! My dad hurt his foot so we can't go and I'll do your chores after I finish ours. My grandparents are coming to the farm for dinner but nothing else is planned. Go ahead and have a good time!"

The picnic plans were on! Things began to fly at the Fischer farm. Dad polished his horseshoes and put them in the trunk of the '36 Chevy. Mother sent the boys to the pig pen for cobs. She lit the cookstove and began making an angel food cake. She told Sylvia to cook potatoes and boil eggs for salad. Mother said, "Tonight we will kill a chicken to fry early in the morning. Sylvia, squeeze some lemons into the gallon thermos and add plenty of sugar. We'll add well water when we leave in the morning!" Timmy and Tommy went in search of a decent ball bat and their baseball.

"We'll take our allowance and buy firecrackers at the park!" Timmy said. Fun was at hand! Dad whispered a prayer, "God bless dependable Walter!"

The family was up early with the hot and shining sun on July 4th. As they gulped their oatmeal, WNAX was predicting a hot, windy day but the Fischer's plans were undaunted. Heat and wind were part of summertime during their life on the prairie. A recording of Sousa's march, "Stars and Stripes Forever" came over the airways and everyone felt like waving a flag. D. B. Gurney himself, acting as announcer, wished everyone a "Happy Day" after which he played the records "America the Beautiful" and "Take Me Out to the Ball Game." Flies buzzed at the screen door until mother tacked up a new fly catcher tape to alleviate the infestation. The scent of chicken frying went all the way to the barn. Custer, the faithful collie dog, hung around the house hoping for scraps of food. The kittens were scratching at the screen door and purring for attention.

The sun got hotter and hotter as it rose in the sky. Sylvia put her hair up in tiny pin curls after wetting the ends with fresh-cooked flax seed. The lotion would insure stiff curls around the brim of her hat. She envisioned ringlets of curls around her face when she met her "Rhett Butler" at the park. At the last minute, she dabbed her precious Evening in Paris perfume behind her ears. It was a special day.

By mid-morning the car was packed with picnic food, a jug of water on board in case the engine heated and the thermos of lemonade and drinking water for the family was loaded. The well at the park was supplied by an artesian well which produced a strange tasting water, so the family brought their own. Before leaving, dad gave each child fifty cents to supplement their saved allowance. This was a small fortune and would buy all the firecrackers, pop, candy and skating tickets necessary for a good celebration. Area businessmen paid for the evening fireworks. It would be a big show if it didn't rain; a remote possibility which would be welcomed by the farmers even more than a big celebration.

The drive to the park was hot and slow, they thought. Timmy claimed Sylvia's perfume made him sick. He said, "I'd rather smell manure." Junior wanted all the windows down but Sylvia was afraid of grasshoppers jumping into the car. She complained that the boys, who each sat at a window, were crushing her skirt. She could feel sweat gathering around the band of her hat but decided to remain silent. "I might meet my Prince Charming today," she dreamed.

To the family's delight, they were able to park under a big tree near a picnic table. The boys ran to find friends, dad headed for the ball diamond and horseshoe pits while mother and Sylvia unloaded the car. They stayed near the picnic table and waited for friends to appear. Sylvia picked a grassy knoll and sat on the grass, spreading her skirt in a circle around her as the catalog model had posed, but it was hot in the sun and no one noticed her. "It will be my luck that only young kids and old men (over 20 years of age) will turn up today. I don't even see girls my age to notice my outfit," she fumed.

Finally, Sylvia decided to check out the crowd for friends. She noticed a family unpacking their car. To her delight she spotted him . . . a boy! A college boy! At least, he wore a white cardigan sweater with a big "W" on the left front. "He must be an athlete. Maybe he'll notice ME!" she hoped. After three more trips past the area and no glances from the young man, she returned to her family for lunch. Mother noticed her lack of friends and consoled, "When roller skating starts at 2 p.m. there will be lots of kids your age." No smile from Sylvia. Her mind was on the "sweater man." Her brain churned out thoughts such as: "I wonder why he wears the sweater on such a hot day? I'll bet he'll be too stuck-up to skate. He's probably going to the dance tonight. Oh, I wish I could stay to dance but the folks will go home right after the fireworks."

Skating time arrived. Sylvia, still wearing her hat, was fitted for skates. She didn't see anyone interesting so skated around the edges to keep from being knocked down by rowdy little kids. The nickelodeon blared "Roll Out the Barrel," "A Tisket-a-Tasket," "My Merry Oldsmobile," and other popular tunes. When her favorite song, "The Skater's Waltz," came over the amplifier, she joined the skaters enjoying the rhythm of it. Suddenly, someone put an arm around her waist and shouted above the din of the crowd, "May I skate with you?" She nearly lost her balance but recovered to notice it was the "sweater man"... sweating and puffing. "Sure!" she nodded. At close range, she noticed his hair was greasy and he smelled strong of perspiration. He had more pimples than the boys in her high school. As he guided her around the turn, he put his hand over his mouth and said, "Hey kid, let's get out of here and have a smoke!" Before she could protest a pack of junior-high boys skated past them with such speed that her hat flew off and rolled across the floor. Several boys grabbed it and then started playing catch with the precious bonnet. Finally, it went rolling across the floor and was run over by a skater.

Her partner laughed at her protests and insisted she leave with him. She broke away and sat on a bench. The boy and his "W" sweater skated away.

Timmy finally rescued the battered bonnet and returned it with brotherly sympathy. The sky blue was streaked with black and the crown was flat as a pancake. Over the loud music an acquaintance skated past and teased, "I'm telling Walter!" This increased her indignity. By this time, the would-be suitor skated past with a blonde girl wearing saddle shoes and a plaid outfit. "I wish I'd stayed home!" she told herself as dust and tears clouded her eyes.

She stayed with her family during the fireworks and shrugged off comfort from friends and family. She had trouble keeping her mouth shut to complain, "It's been a rotten day!"

Enroute home, she laid her crushed hat in the back window of the car and sat huddled in the corner trying to catch a breath of air. Timmy and Junior were full of stories while mom and dad exchanged news they had heard.

As dad turned the corner near their farm, a whirlwind of air swept through the car, sweeping the hat with it . . . it flew through the window into the night like a flying object disappearing into the beyond . . . gone from sight . . . gone with the wind! Sylvia let out a shriek. Her family tried to subdue their laughter.

As dad drove toward the farm, they spotted a light. "What could that be?" dad remarked. Driving closer, they noticed the big farm lantern sitting on the porch steps. Beside the lit lantern sat Walter petting Custer. "My goodness," Mother worried, "Something is wrong. He should be home by now." They all rushed toward Walter and he explained, " . . . thought I'd hang around to tell you that Clem, your new hired hand, will be here the first thing in the morning. I answered your telephone tonight. Oh, yes, and the grey cat has a batch of kittens in the barn."

The boys let out a hoot and ran to the barn to visit the newborns. Mother and dad hauled the picnic stuff into the house. Sylvia stood in amazement... speechless. Walter took the quiet opportunity, grabbed her around the waist and gave her a big kiss! She was too startled to say a word.

Without waiting for a response, Walter untied his horse from the garden post, mounted and rode down the lane. He yelled, "Happy Fourth of July" as he galloped away leaving a cloud of dust behind.

Sylvia stood affixed to the porch steps. She petted Custer, took a deep breath and touched her lips. "Well, it wasn't such a bad day at that... but he didn't even get to see my hat!"

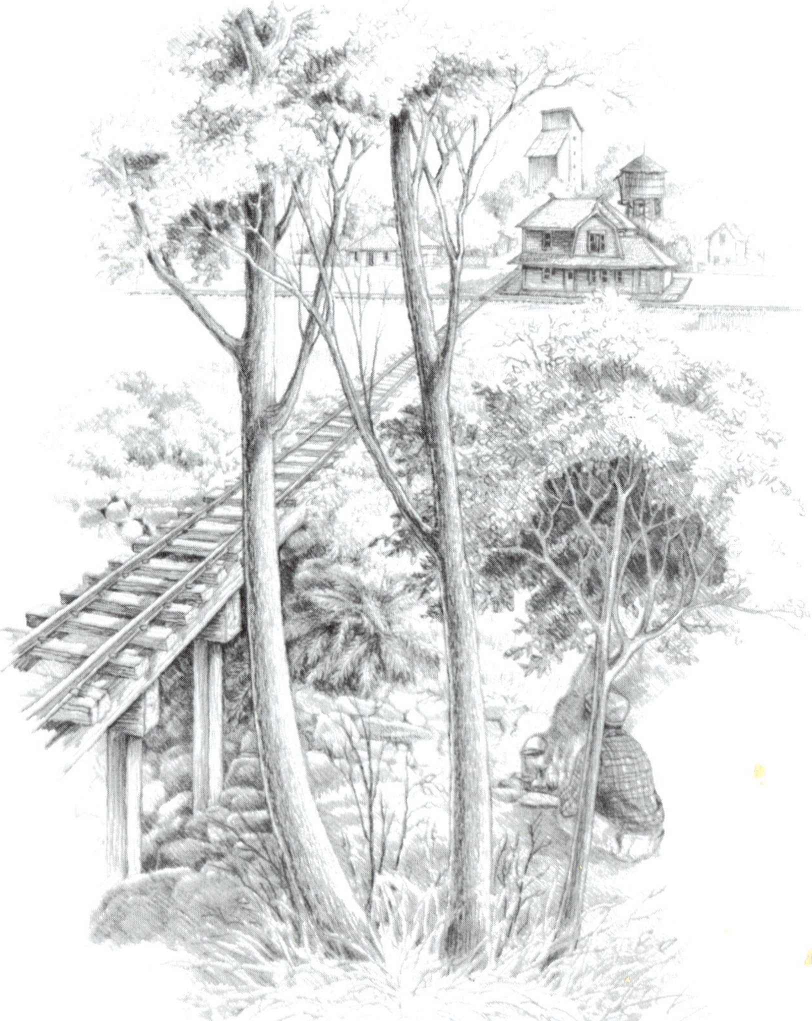
Coppock
© 1989

Homeless Hobos

Today street people of every kind roam our cities. Headlines talk of the thousands of homeless Americans. These vagrants are often addicted to liquor and drugs, suffer mental problems or are suspects in robbery and assault cases. No one trusts them. This was not true of the nomads and homeless of my childhood. Fifty years ago the homeless can be remembered with nostalgic and picturesque pleasure. They were the hobos; sometimes called bums and tramps. They rode the railroad boxcars, crisscrossing the country without rhyme and reason. They did not care where they had been nor where they were going. These restless men (I never heard of a female hobo) would catch a ride on a moving train, jump between the cars or into an empty boxcar (a covered railroad car with sliding doors used for hauling cargo) riding until they were evicted or hungry. They would then jump off the train near a town and beg for food from house to house. They were sober and harmless. Railroad officials usually ignored them as long as they did not interfere with railroad business. When they were satisfied with food and water, they would hop another train and travel from place to place—someplace—anyplace, talking to fellow hobos, begging food and living in what was called the Railroad Jungle.

These jungle retreats were hobo-made semi-shelters near the railroad tracks. They were often under bridges or along any tree-covered area. Here they built open fires with whatever wood, paper or coal they could find in the vicinity. Sometimes they could find coal which had fallen off the coal cars used to fuel the steam engine. They warmed themselves and made mulligan stew from vegetables they had begged, heated beans (5 cents per can) and made coffee in tin cans or crude pots. They rested and visited with other wanderers, smoked and sometimes slept overnight waiting for a train. Often they had no idea where the train was headed except in winter they traveled southbound and in the summer they traveled northbound since weather was a factor in their outdoor existence.

There were many bums and hobos riding the trains in the southern states as the climate was warm and outdoor living was tolerable. Train officials did not treat them as kindly as northern hobos since they were considered a nuisance and a fire hazard because of their smoking in boxcars and tending cooking fires along the railroad tracks. They were often evicted from the cars before the trains departed the station but these men were adept at jumping onto a moving train and riding on top or in any space they could find. This included the truss-rods which were mounted under the cars to stabilize and hold the floor rigid. They would lay boards across the rods and ride. However, this was very dangerous and many of them lost legs or were killed in accidents in this manner.

It was a losing battle in the South to keep the bums off the trains. Many of the southern men were called "Yeggs" as they were armed and dangerous criminals. These men seldom traveled in the north since the warm weather was a short season and the midwestern territory was not suitable for their lifestyle. In the Dakotas, hobos were seldom involved in a crime. Sometimes they were picked up by the police and spent the night in jail as "vagrants" but they enjoyed the bed and food. In talking with retired railroad personnel, they agreed the travelers in the prairie states were mainly adventurous men without homes or jobs.

A typical small Dakota town was a favorite stop for hobos, Wentworth, South Dakota. People claimed Wentworth to be the smallest town in the country with a Union depot; meaning there were two railroad lines served by one depot and station agent. The Great Northern Railroad ran through the town north and south while the Milwaukee Road traversed the area east and west. Railroad crews, section hands who maintained the tracks, and other train personnel lived in Wentworth and nearby Madison, South Dakota. The railroad supported three large grain elevators in Wentworth as well as the auxiliary businesses which made it a prosperous, small town. An average of sixteen trains a day passed through this Lake County town. Most of the trains, during the warm season, carried hobos who were riding the rails. It was fun for the local teenagers to join the drayman, who hauled goods in a horse-drawn wagon to and from the trains for local businesses; the mail truck and a few passengers, boarding and deboarding, to watch the action at the depot. Locals waved at the conductor and the engineer and they waved back. They waved at the men in the caboose, the last car of the train, and speculated where the hobos were going. Some had jumped off to go begging for food in town while others from earlier trains jumped on as soon as the train whistle blew indicating it was leaving the station. Some trains had a few boxcars plus the passenger cars and were short trains while others stretched up to a half mile. It was entertaining to sit on the train platform or stand on the depot's wooden deck and watch the switchmen sidetrack some car to leave for the future. Watching the night trains come in was full of drama. Train headlights could be seen coming from a distance of several miles and the series of whistles meaning the train was approaching the station and preparing to stop could be heard all over the town. The lights were glaring and intense, so hobos could be seen jumping off the railroad cars, their silhouettes reflecting in the moonlight. They would land in the ditch and disappear in the tree-lined thicket. The local hobo jungle was near a railroad bridge on the far edge of town.

When the conversation was dull, locals would fantasize the romantic and mysterious life of these beggars. They talked about the stories heard of Hobo Conventions held in New Orleans where they elected a "King of Tramps." They speculated on the remote chance of their nobility visiting this area. Could they be recognized? Would they give autographs? It was fun to contemplate this possibility.

Hobos never begged at night but in the morning they would rap on back doors of homes and stores. When a woman answered they would say, "Lady, can you spare a poor guy a loaf of bread or some tobacco?" The kind-hearted woman usually found some food which was termed a "hand-out." The man would mumble, "thanks" and continue his route. It was rumored that they had a secret marking code and knew which houses could be depended upon to hand out "grub," a hobo jargon for food.

Grandma must have had a mark on her door but it was not noticeable. She never refused a man food or clothing. She was typical of many kind-hearted first generation immigrants who would provide food such as potatoes, bread, coffee or leftovers from the kitchen.

A Personal Recollection:

One warm summer day a group of friends and I, unbeknown to our parents, explored the hobo jungle down by the tracks. It was an adventure planned for some time. We surveyed the scene at a distance to make sure no hobos were camping there. This area was along a deep ravine under a railroad bridge. Large, straggly cottonwood trees provided shade and protection from prairie winds. We explored the plot where the activity had been most evident. All we found, to our disappointment, was a pile of rusty tin cans, mostly pork and beans, ashes from long-dead fires and assorted pieces of newspapers from faraway places. Apparently, the men carried every bit of paraphernalia, such as cooking supplies and extra clothing in their gunny sacks. The romantic version of a hobo with a red knapsack on the end of a long stick slung over their shoulder was a myth. The honest-to-goodness tramp of the 1930s was a raggedly dressed man carrying heavy loads of worldly goods. The mystery of what might be in their sacks produced visions of fantastic possibilities we would never know. No two men dressed alike. They wore several layers of pants or overalls, ragged shirts and jackets and a hat of some description. They were all hungry and thirsty when they begged at doors but most towns had a city water pump in a park or near the depot so they could get drinking water.

One hot August afternoon, I was home alone when a hobo knocked on the back door. He had the usual plea, "Lady, can you spare a hungry man a bite to eat?" I was 15-years-old at the time and was used to cooking as my parents both worked in our family grocery store. I told him to wait on the back porch, I found some meat for a sandwich, some cookies which had seen their better days and gave him a pitcher of lemonade. He sat on the back step and ate with gusto. I asked him why he didn't work and he said, "cuz I can't git none." I told him, "You can mow our lawn. I'll give you fifty cents and more food." He finished eating and agreed. He followed me into the garage where I pulled out our old lawn mower. In those days, mowers were hand-push affairs with a rotary blade which turned to cut the grass. Our house was on a corner lot so there was a big yard and the grass was also quite high due to a recent rain.

The man began mowing. I kept an eye on him all afternoon as he mowed, wiped his face with an old red bandanna, drank water and mowed more. By late afternoon, he came to the back door and reported he had finished. He also grunted, "Yer mower is sure dull!" I paid him the fifty cents and gave him a sack of vegetables. The hobo wanted to know where my Dad was, thinking he should have a little more money. I pointed him toward town and told him to stop at the grocery store. I telephoned my Dad and explained the situation. Dad was happy because he thought he'd have to mow the lawn after supper. When the tramp came into the store, Dad gave him a can of Copenhagen tobacco, a tin of Sir Walter Raleigh, a plug of Red Star and a corn cob pipe which had been on the shelf as long as I could remember. Dad said the happy hobo grinned from ear to ear. When Dad threw in some candy bars, the tramp mumbled some more "thank-yous" and trudged toward the railroad tracks. He disappeared into the hot August sunset to board the next train north. In the heat of the 1930s, one couldn't get too far north.

For some reason, we didn't have more hobos stop at our back door that summer. Maybe we did have a secret mark that told them of our dull lawn mower. None of us ever gave it a thought that it wasn't safe for a young girl to be home alone feeding a tramp.

In talking to numerous railroad men who worked the trains in the area fifty years ago, they agreed that these men were seldom violent. Paul Redfield, a retired engineer from Madison, South Dakota, said he never knew one he was afraid of after seeing hundreds of these freeloaders. He once asked a hobo, "Where are you going?" The guy scratched his head and replied, "Well, I'll be damned if I know where a man should go!"

Mr. Redfield says one tramp must have owned a very sharp knife as he had carved on every wooden railroad water tower and other buildings in this part of the country, He carved, "TEX" and under it, "K.T.", meaning "King of Tramps."

Verald Westby, also a retired railroad man from Madison, South Dakota, recalls hobos covered themselves with newspapers for insulation against cold and dampness. They put sacks over their feet and in their boots during the winter. Mr. Westby recalls, "The best coffee I ever drank in my life was some a hobo cooked over a bonfire in a three-pound coffee can and I drank it out of a tin can." He commented, "My wife couldn't make coffee that tasted that good."

After World War II the hobos met their demise. Railroad authorities did not put up with their riding and people no longer fed them. Social agencies were funded to help the homeless so the beggars became a thing of the past. I haven't seen a tramp in forty years. I haven't seen a train for a while either.

We sometimes envied these Knights of the Road for their freedom but more often we pitied them for being without home and family or the comforts of the lives we lived in 1930-1945. Hobos were beckoned toward the evasive pot-of-gold envisioned at the end of the rainbow. The perspective of the narrowing parallel rails of steel promised a destination they never found; hobos are now just a picturesque memory in our history.

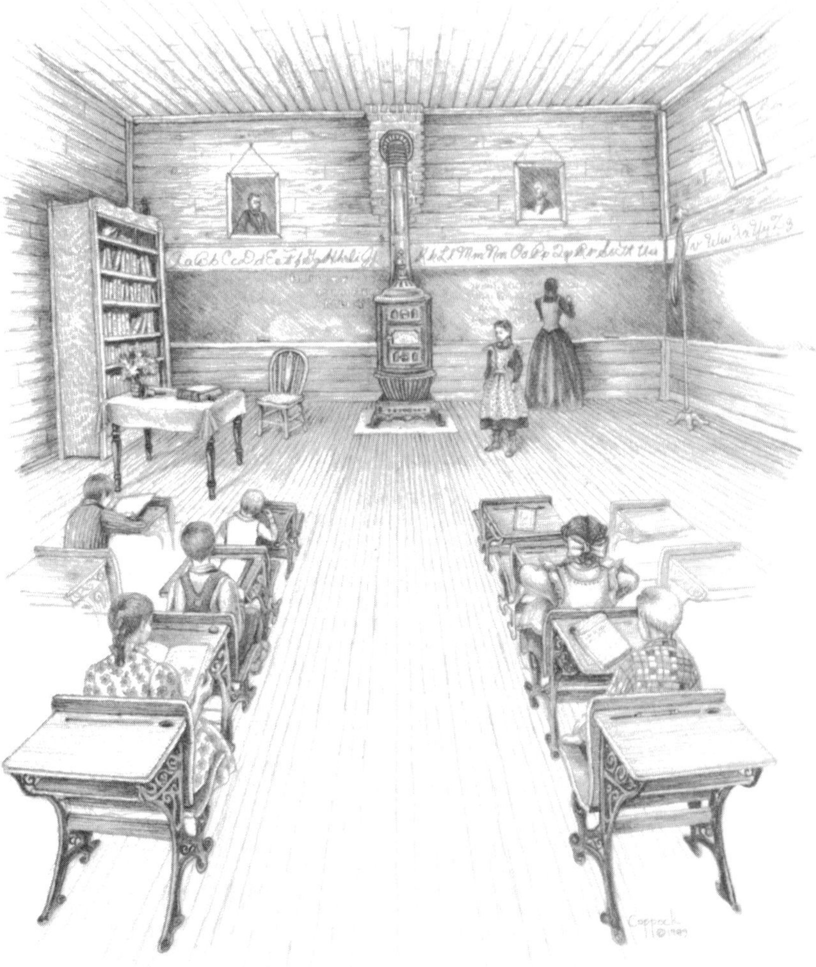
Coppock

Harold Goes to School

"Harold Goes to School" is a true adventure story of a small child in rural McCook County, South Dakota in the year 1916.

Harold and his brother, Marion, are sons of the late Mr. and Mrs. Chellis Hamaker, farmers in the Spencer, South Dakota area. Harold is a former band director at Mitchell High School and is now retired and residing in Mitchell, South Dakota. He is still active in church and civic organizations. His brother, Marion, has retired from farming in McCook County and resides in Spencer, South Dakota.

The teacher, Miss Burmester, is still living. Her married name is Mrs. Hester Goins. She is 94 years old and resides in Spencer, South Dakota. She taught schools in McCook County for many years.

The story depicts a child's desires and gives a picture of rural school life in South Dakota almost 70 years ago.

HAROLD GOES TO SCHOOL

Harold opened his eyes to the warm May sunshine streaking through his window. He quickly closed them again and sank deeper into the warmth of his feather bed mattress. Before he dared open them again he reasoned, "Is this the day? Is this really the long awaited day when I will be going to school?"

Actually Harold was aware he was much too young to trod the mile down the country road to the Benton School where his older brother, Marion, spent his days and came home with exciting tales of the hours spent in the white clapboard building located at the far end of their farmstead.

Marion was already in Second Primer and was at least a head taller than Harold. Marion had celebrated his seventh birthday. Marion told Harold his birthday would not come for many months and then Harold would be five years old.

But Harold was going to school on this May day in 1916. He was going to see the inside of the building which held such fascination for him.

His brother had told him about a wonderful gadget which was attached to the wall in the back of the room. One could put a brown penny pencil in the hole on the side, turn the handle rapidly and the pencil point came out as sharp as mother's darning needle. It was so sharp that one had to take extra care not to tear the paper of his nickel tablet while he figured sums.

Marion told him the hard little eraser could also be sharpened in this amazing machine called a pencil sharpener but the eraser was made of a stiff gray substance and broke easily the first time it was used. Sharpening the eraser was fun but not a very good idea. How fun it would be to give that machine a few turns, mused Harold.

He came out of his day dreams and jumped out of bed onto the cool linoleum floor. He raced to the kitchen to make sure this was really the day the entire family would be going to the last day of school for the "end of school year" picnic.

Harold's mother was busy rolling pie crusts on the big pine table and the teakettle was singing on the back of the big Home Comfort cook stove. The pungent smell of baking bread seeped from the oven.

Ma told him to hurry and dress but to put on his work coveralls as there was much to be done before the school picnic adventure. Just then Pa came in the back door with two large galvanized pails brimming with foamy white milk. He set them by the cream separator and poured himself a cup of coffee from the blue speckled pot which was simmering on the back of the range. Pa reached into the wood box and threw a few cobs into the fire.

Pa told Harold to wake Marion so the boys could eat their oatmeal and then pick enough cobs in the pig pen so Ma could keep the range fire going to bake her apple pies. They could take the two bushel baskets in the red wagon to haul them and make quick work of this chore. By this time Marion was dressed and ready for his oatmeal which was plopping in the kettle near the water reservoir. Harold ran to the bedroom to dress but returned to the kitchen for his mother to help him lace his boots.

As the boys picked the dry cobs, Marion told Harold the school picnic would really be fun! The boys finished filling the baskets, unloaded the cobs into the wood bin near the stove, and went out to the barn to feed Tubby the cat and Old Shep their dog.

They picked some dandelions and violets on their way into the house and gave them to Ma for a table centerpiece.

By 11:30, Dad had cranked up his new Buick touring car, Ma had loaded the back with her hamper of fried chicken, fresh buns, pies and a jug of lemonade.

Dad would drive home after lunch to get a chunk of ice from the grain bin and bring the ice cream freezer. Ma had mixed the eggs, milk and sugar to make the ice cream and had hung it in the well to keep cool before leaving for the picnic. The combination would become the freezer of home-made ice cream to be served in the late afternoon. The men would sit around the freezer, mix chopped ice and salt for the freezing and take turns cranking the handle on the side of the wooden bucket freezer. They would enjoy that chore.

When they arrived at the school, Harold was first to scramble out of the car and bounce off the running board. He ran to a spot in the shade on the west side of the school house. Women were already laying food and dishes out on a table for the big meal. Kids were running on the hillside, chasing each other, yelling and laughing. Harold and Marion saw the neighbor children and joined in the frolic.

After the big picnic meal of beans, buns, chicken, cabbage salad, pie, pickles, lemonade and enough goodies to boggle the small mind, it was time for fun and games.

Actually Harold ate very little as his mind was on the freezer of ice cream which had long been in his day dreams.

The kids spent the afternoon playing games organized by the teacher, Miss Burmester. They played tag, kick-the-can, hide-and-seek, "Captain May I?" and a dozen other running and sitting games.

Harold kept his eye on the ice cream freezer and before long the men, who had been turning the crank, began unpacking the ice on the top. They removed the dasher, which was coated with frosty ice cream, just as Harold arrived to watch. The men gave Harold a spoon to lick and taste the wonderful elixir which clung to the dasher. The men then packed more ice on top to allow the mixture to "ripen," they said.

Since the day was sunny and bright, no one suggested going into the school house so the four-year-old could not see the inside of this mysterious institution on picnic day.

By four o'clock, the ice cream was sufficiently ripened and ready for eating. The men were talking about getting home to bring the milk cows into the barn for milking, feed the hogs and the horses. The women gave thought to their chicken chores and the evening meal but continued to exchange recipes and small talk.

The magic moment came! The women had spread left-over food such as pies, cakes and cookies on the table. The men unpacked the ice cream and spooned it into white bowls. Harold was first in line even though his mother had told him to stay back until the big people had their treat.

The ice cream was wonderful—every bit the dream he had dreamed—and he licked the dish shiny clean.

It was a tired, but happy boy who climbed into his dad's auto for the trip home.

That night he lay deep in his feather bed and he decided, "No matter what—I'm going to school next year!"

August came and Marion was excited about his new pencil and tablet. He could scarcely wait for his first day in third grade. Secretly Harold knew he was going to school also, as he wanted more of the homemade ice cream.

The first day of school finally arrived and Marion proudly trudged down the road with his syrup pail full of lunch and his new school supplies.

Harold's mother went into the summer kitchen to can tomatoes. She told her small son to play in the house while she worked. As soon as she disappeared, Harold plopped on his little straw hat and started down the road toward school as fast as his legs would carry him. He had nearly reached the school when the neighbor, who was cutting hay across the road, stopped his team of horses and yelled at Harold. He told Harold, "You run right home or I'll catch you and tie you up!"

Harold started toward home and then ran into the cornfield. He lost his straw hat but doubled back through the corn rows and continued to run toward the school yard. He crossed the playground and then crept up the four wooden steps to the school door. His mouth was drooling with the thought of homemade ice cream which they may be ready to serve or maybe they would eat it at noontime! He also thought of the fun he would have in school.

The screen door was slightly ajar as he slowly opened it and eased his way past the row of lunch pails on the entry floor. All was quiet! He peered into the room and surveyed the scene. All the kids, who had been running so fast at the picnic were sitting quietly in rows of desks with their heads bent over reading books.

Miss Burmester was making marks on the chalkboard and her back was turned away from the class. She stood erectly and spoke sternly.

There were pictures of two men, one on each side of the wall, peering down on the silent group. These must be the pictures of Lincoln and Washington that Marion had told him were important presidents. The American flag hung limp on a pole in the corner. No one twirling the handle of the shiny pencil sharpening machine.

There was no ice cream in sight! Not a single cake! And the children weren't laughing.

Harold quietly slipped out of the door. He thought about his adventure and decided, "I guess I'll stay home this year and enjoy mother's warm kitchen and tasty cookies."

At that very moment, he could see his father's auto heading up the dusty road toward the schoolhouse.

Halloweens Past

GHOST NIGHT, 1935:
The year was 1935. The local football team was top in the conference, which made the coach and players proud. As Halloween approached, the coach had a serious locker room talk with his players. He told the team to keep their image even though Halloween prompted a temptation to do a little devilment around the town. "We've got the townfolks proud of us now so don't mess it up by putting a manure spreader on the mayor's porch!" he lectured them.

Carl and Joe, 16-year-old defensive backs for the team, were anxious for action on the forthcoming Devil's Night. They had been conjuring up ideas for fun on Halloween. The coach's admonition put a hole in their balloon. They maybe better watch it, they thought.

Halloween night provided a full moon, warm weather, and gentle breezes. The night was right for funning! Carl and Joe talked it over and decided they had better lay low this year. They agreed to walk uptown, stop in the Sugar Bowl, a local teenage hangout, and watch the little kids soap windows and throw tin cans. It was a far cry from their original plans for the night. Since the boys had just gotten their new letterman's football jackets with a big "F" on the front, they decided to wear their blue and gold to show off a little. "Gotta have a little jazz," they said.

By ten o'clock the street was littered with junk, the little kids had gone home to count their loot and the action on main street was down to zero. Halloween night would come and go without any contributions from the two football jocks. It hardly seemed fair.

As they sipped their third Cokes in the back booth of the cafe and contemplated their plight, a couple of their high school friends burst in the back door and whispered to them, "Hey, old man Larson just turned off his light and went to bed." "It's time to dump his outhouse!" Carl and Joe shrugged to each other with desolate expressions. "It's tradition," they were thinking. "We ALWAYS dump Larson's outhouse! It wouldn't be Halloween without it!"

Simultaneously, they jumped out of the booth. Coke glasses, straws and candy wrappers scattered as they raced out the back door to join their fellow pranksters. They hopped on the fender of Bill's tin lizzie and sped to the Larson place on the edge of town. It would be a "hit and run" affair, they thought.

They stopped the old Ford in the lane and jumped out. Joe and Carl bounded off the fender and were the first to reach the gleaming white building. How nice it looked in the moonlight! They ran to the site, put strong football-trained shoulders to the building and gave their best effort. It was like pushing through for a touchdown... only something was different.

The building did not budge enough to tip, but they felt a sticky wet something on their hands and jackets. Old man Larson had out-foxed them. He'd put a nice new coat of Hardware Olson's #1 white lead paint on the outhouse in the late afternoon. The oil-based paint was still wet and made a great impression on Carl and Joe... at least on their pants and jackets.

Old man Larson peeked out the window and had the laugh of the year. His own Halloween trick had paid off!

GHOST NIGHT, 1945:

Two small rural towns, Fletcher and Roscoe, had been rivals as far back as anyone could remember. Fletcher was the county seat and larger than Roscoe, six miles away, but due to consolidation of school districts and the rural bus systems, the enrollment of the two schools was not greatly different.

The competition between the sports teams was always to a point of mayhem. Roscoe students said Fletcher kids called them "stuck-up." Fletcher kids called the Roscoe students "small town hicks" and a few more things. Rivalry was always evident, but especially on Halloween. What damage was done in either town was blamed on the kids from the other. Those were the days when most towns had only one police officer and he was easily decoyed on the big night of pranks.

For years, it had been Fletcher's fun to tip over the large community out-house which stood in the Roscoe city park on the edge of main street. It sometimes took a full scale plan to get the job done and sometimes they failed. If the building was tipped on Halloween, the Roscoe high school boys were sent to the park during the school noon hour the next day to set it up. This was a sore spot to say the least.

This year Roscoe had a plan! They were not going to be tricked again. Since Halloween fell on a Saturday night the Roscoe boys met in the park early evening to instigate their plan. They carefully and skillfully moved the building three feet back of the footings. They then covered the open excavation with branches and leaves. It was a perfect trap.

In order to witness the event, the boys took a long ladder, climbed to the top of the nearby fire hall roof, which was flat, pulled the ladder up behind them and waited. It was a long and cold wait. They almost decided to abandon the vigil thinking their plans had been in vain.

About eleven o'clock, the shivering boys heard a car speeding down the hill toward town. In a matter of minutes the car unloaded a half dozen Fletcher young men who raced to the sight of the building to do the dastardly deed.

"Crack! Crunch! Pop! Plunk!" Leaves and branches gave away as the boys fell into the pit. Language of various descriptions of vulgarity emitted from them as they crawled to safety, wiped their feet, and did what they could to recover.

By this time, the Roscoe boys were standing on the fire house roof laughing and shouting. They had developed the master plan. The trap had worked!

The next spring the PTA put in concrete foundations and new, improved city outhouses. The fun was over but never forgotten.

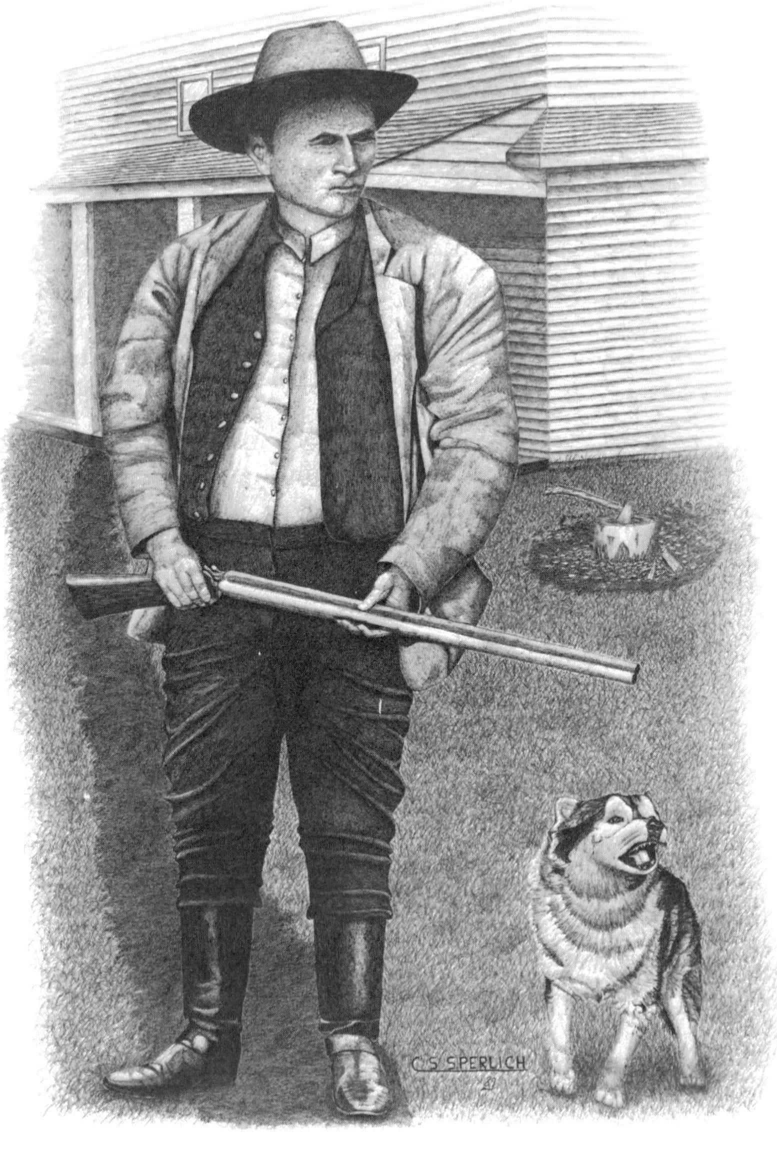
C.S. SPERLICH

Who's in the Hen House

When the telephone rang fifteen long-short rings (called a General Ring) at 11 p.m. on a cold, moonlit night, everybody jumped out of bed to answer. The telephone operator, termed "Central," waited patiently until she heard at least ten "hellos" to announce. "Chicken thieves have just sacked the Bloomberg's hen house. The thieves are driving a small coupe and traveling west from Bloomberg's farm. Try to make a road block at the Badger corner if it's not too late!" Repeat: "Chicken thieves ...

Receivers clicked and every man on the phone circuit jumped into his coveralls, raced to the garage to crank up the car and drove toward the site of the intended trap to catch the culprits.

As the men dashed off, some forgetting to take their shotguns, the women on the party line began to discuss the details of the crime. Older children, now wide awake, lit the lamps, put fuel in the stoves and peered out the windows into the moonlight. Some secretly thought, "How come we never have chicken thieves or some big excitement?"

Stealing of precious poultry was a capital sin as far as prairie farmers viewed the crime. In addition to the financial loss, the chickens belonged to MOTHER! She took great pride in hatching eggs for the little chicks and tending them until they were good layers and a reliable food source for winter. It was usually "a chicken in every pot" on Sundays.

In fact, President Herbert Hoover had promised, "A car in every garage and a chicken in every pot" during his campaign. It hadn't turned out that way. The drought of the '30s was taking its toll on the crops, grasshoppers devastated the area and prices for produce, stock, corn and grain were at rock bottom. The era was termed, "The Great Depression."

On the Saturday night following the Bloomberg raid most farm families were "in town" to do their trading, selling eggs in return for groceries or tokens and selling cream and churned butter. The men went to the barber shop for hair cuts (sometimes the luxury of a shave) in anticipation of the weekend which involved church and possible visitors. It was mid-November so the harvest was finished and there was time to catch up on the social news of the area.

Since it was too cold to sit in cars or stand on the sidewalks to visit with friends and neighbors, the women congregated around the pot-bellied stoves in the town's grocery stores. The men drifted between the cream station, gas station, barber shop, pool hall and fire hall, where there was usually a game of whist in progress.

Bertha Larsen had the attention of one group since her chicken coop was the latest to be raided. She told her story with great excitement. "We were sound asleep when we heard Duke, our dog, whimpering in the kitchen. Adolph got up to let Duke out. Duke then started barking up a storm and running toward the chicken house. By that time the kids and I were looking out the upstairs windows and saw a couple of men with gunny sacks under their arms, running down the lane. There was just enough moonlight to see them jump into a car parked near the driveway. They didn't turn on their headlights as they sped down the gravel road. Adolph grabbed his old blunderbuss of a shotgun but couldn't find the shells. He jumped in the car and drove after them. The kids and I were sure scared! Adolph came back in a few minutes and said there was so much dust at the mile road he couldn't see which way they turned. We called Central to place a general ring but it was too late to catch them, we knew."

Almost breathless, Bertha continued, "Harry Downs and Joe Olson heard the General Ring right away and drove to the Johnson corner but didn't see a thing so they went back home. They were outfoxed by those terrible men!"

Olga Johnson finally got a word in edgewise to comment, "Yes, and broilers are worth 15 cents a pound now! How many did they steal?"

Bertha replied, "As near as we know they stole about a dozen of the Rhode Island reds I have in the south chicken house! I'd sure like to get my hands on those guys!"

By this time, each woman was giving a report on someone who had had a like experience this past summer or fall. Mary Lewis reported, "My sister, who lives in Miner County, said there has been a rash of chicken stealing there, too. Almost every Saturday night, when everyone is in town, some family comes home to find their poultry gone. They even took ducks and geese over there."

She continued to relate, "My sister said that at one farm the old rooster must have made so much noise that the thieves rung his neck and threw him out of the pen. The dog must have drug him away and they didn't find him until the next day!"

The stories of poultry pilfering went on and on . . . the little kids were fascinated and also afraid so they stayed close to their parents. The older children were tired of hearing the same tales every place.

The men in the pool hall were speculating as to who might be the thief or thieves since the robbers seemed to know when people were gone. After much speculation, over bottles of Grain Belt, they decided that the recent thefts were the work of a local person or gang.

Harvey Lewis said some strong words and vowed, "... ##&&$**. Also, ...! if I ever catch one on my farm I'll tar and feather him!" Names of possible culprits were thrown out, such as: "Could be Stubby Jones as he always has plenty of pocket money!"

"Naw," Billy Burke retorted, "He's always drinking beer in the card room on Saturday nights when the coops are raided! Besides, he's a 'chicken' himself!" At this remark the men standing along the bar laughed and slammed their bottles down in emphasis.

"What about the Casperson kid? He has to pay for that new '32 Ford someway!" Lewis snarled. Several men came to Casperson's rescue, "He always goes to Spring Valley to visit his girlfriend on Saturday nights!" They all agreed to that statement.

At the cream station, several were waiting for their cream to be tested so they could get their checks. The conversation came around to chicken business after discussing the early frost and the cold November temperatures.

Several expressed their opinions on the possible guilty persons. Albert Parker remarked, "We've been laying for the crooks. My son, Johnnie, has an ag project at school. His project is the fifty Leghorns he's raising on the farm. Some of them will top the scale at five pounds! They better not hit our place! I'd fill their pants full of lead if I caught them on my land!" he vowed.

A group of teenagers were warming up around the stove in the Hurry-Scurry Cafe and Restaurant. A few were lucky enough to have a nickel and were enjoying fountain Cokes at the round tables in the front of the cafe. At one of the back booths Zack Jammison had the makings for home-rolled cigarettes and was treating his pals to a smoke. A fifty-cent pitcher of beer was another treat he was providing the boys who were old enough to imbibe in a public place. There was such laughter and noise in the booth that the waitress warned them to quiet down.

After talk of the basketball game with Stubbenville, in which the home team had lost 20-10, the discussion of plans for the Thanksgiving party, the chicken thief problem was debated by a high school group seated at the big middle table.

"Who would be so brave as to steal chickens from the hen houses?" they wondered. Some expressed an opinion that it was "risky business" while others thought it would be "easy money." Since the crowd knew most of the young people in the area, they concluded it had to be some punks from Sioux Falls who were hungry for beer money. Also they would have a better chance of selling the loot. The crowd at the cafe broke up about nine o'clock when families began leaving for home.

On the Saturday night before Thanksgiving, Otto Kroeger was coming down with a bad cold. He told the family to go to town without him. He said, "I'll stay home and soak my feet in Epsom Salts!"

Billy, who was sixteen, said he'd drive the truck to town so they could sell cream and mother could take her churned butter to sell. Mother agreed, "I heard on the party line that Kramer's Store has fresh cranberries and yams for sale. They would sure round out the Thanksgiving menu. Also, I'm out of sage since the Watkins man didn't call this month. If the eggs bring enough I can buy some fruit for Thanksgiving... some oranges and bananas."

The little kids said they could ride in the back as they wanted to see some friends in town. It was a good plan.

Otto was listening to the Delco battery radio and enjoying Amos and Andy and hadn't realized it was getting late. He then became engrossed in Fibber McGee and Molly and hadn't bothered to light the kerosene lamps. It was almost nine o'clock when he heard a car drive up the lane and turn off the engine near the chicken coop. He thought this was strange. He hurriedly put on his shoes and work coat. As a last minute thought, he grabbed the shotgun off the shelf in the parlor.

By this time the dog was yapping to get out of the house yard fence and Otto knew he had a problem... chicken thieves! He let the dog out with a "sic 'em!" Before Otto could get to the hen house, a shadow emerged from the building with a gunny sack of sqawking chickens protesting to get out. The figure was illuminated by the pale moonlight. The man threw the gunny sack into the back of his car. Simultaneously Otto aimed a blast of his double barrelled shotgun in the man's behind. The culprit let out a howl, jumped into his vehicle and sped down the lane. Otto kept trying to pump lead into the tires of the get-away car.

As soon as Otto ran to the house he called Central and asked for a General Ring on the telephone. She immediately rang the party-line code. As "hellos" came on the line she reported: "Chicken thieves have just struck at the Kroeger farm! He thinks they are traveling east. Be on the look-out! Repeat: Chicken thieves..."

He then rang two shorts and a long ring for Kramer's Store and reported the theft. He told the clerk to tell his missus and also find the sheriff, who was usually playing cards in Ben's card room next to the store.

At this time the family, who were already enroute home, arrived to hear the devastating news. Mother immediately took the lantern to check her broilers and found at least ten missing. She "clucked and clucked" her tongue to think there were such dishonest people in the world as to steal her precious chickens.

About 10 p.m. that Saturday night there was an urgent knocking on Dr. Thompson's front door. A young man, who appeared to be in pain, asked the doctor to help him. He said, "I was coon hunting along the county line when I was shot from behind! I think I have shot in my seat. It hurts like hell! I'm in real pain, Doc, can you take them out?"

Doc hurriedly dressed and took the young man to his deserted office where he spent considerable time removing the shot and coating the wounds with iodine while the patient moaned and groaned.

The following day Doc Thompson reported the incident to the county sheriff as it was a law that all gunshot wounds be reported to the authorities. With the evidence of the gunshot wounds and Otto Kroeger's testimony along with the chicken feathers found in the back of Zack Jammison's car, the case was strong enough to indict the 21-year-old man who confessed to the Kroeger incident as well as several others.

At the trial, two weeks later, in the county court house the testimony was presented. The judge pronounced the sentence with little hesitation: "I sentence Zack Jammison to seven years in the State Penitentiary, non-commutable sentence! Court dismissed!"

This was the harsh penalty in the 1930s for raiding Mother's sacred chicken house. Her hens provided eggs and poultry to feed the family plus the all-important egg money to buy necessities of life, and one sentencing put an end to chicken thieving for a while.

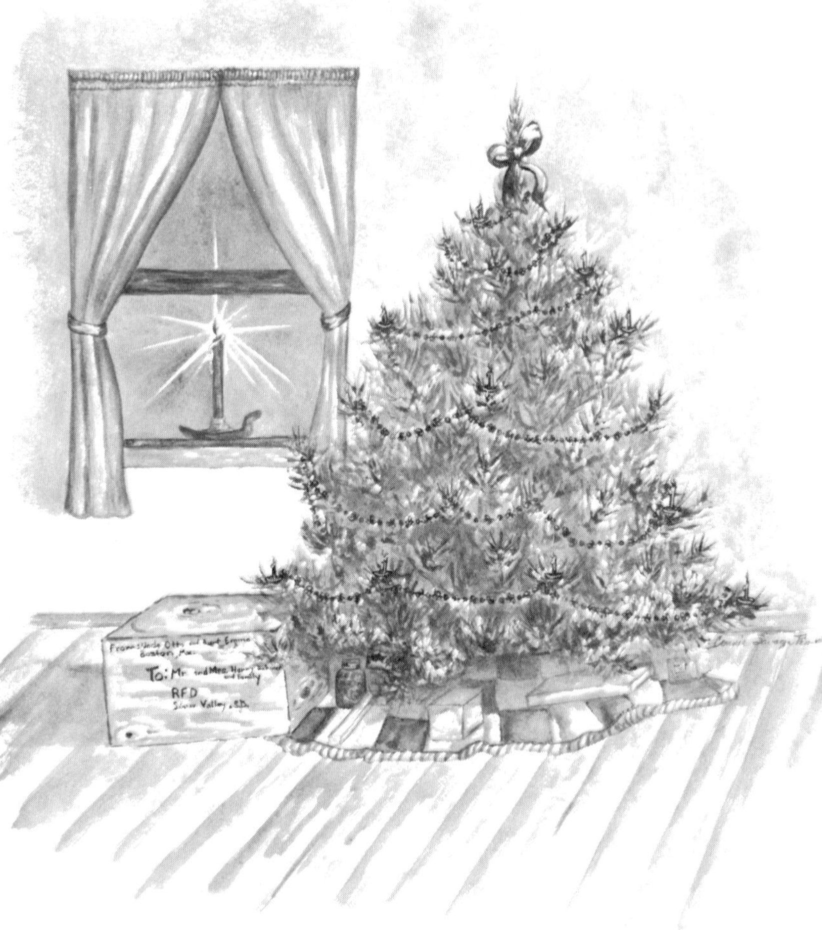
To: Mr.
RFD

The Christmas Box

The Dahlmeyer family had been watching the rural mail box for days in anticipation of the annual Christmas package which they expected from Aunt Emma and Uncle Otto, who lived in Boston. These distant relatives had no children of their own, but they always remembered their kinfolk who lived on what they termed "The Prairies of South Dakota."

Aunt Emma's letters indicated she believed South Dakota to be an uncivilized country. Deep down, Aunt Emma knew that was not true but she embroidered this idea when she told her friends about her poor relatives. She felt the least Otto and she could do for her brother, sister-in-law and their seven children was to provide a little pleasure for them during the holiday season.

Henry Dahlmeyer, Emma's brother, had a different picture of rural life. He loved the farm scene. He told his friends that he had left "a noisy, industrial mass of people" for the open spaces and clean air of the west. Henry and Sarah were happy with their farm which was located on the eastern edge of South Dakota. It was a wonderful place to raise a family.

The year was 1935 and there was a shortage of rainfall. But, the family was happy the grasshopper plague and dust storms of western South Dakota had left them on the very edge of these problems. Money was in short supply but there was plenty of hay and grain for the animals and the garden yielded an adequate supply of fruit and vegetables.

Aunt Emma wrote to her nieces and nephews several times during the year and described the wonderful stores in Boston. She told them of the giant Bloomingdale's Department Store and the fascinating Woolworth's "Five and Dime" store. The Woolworth store brought most of the daydreams to the older girls who dreamed someday they could board the Milwaukee Railroad train to visit these elderly relatives. Until that day, however, they settled for dreams of such magic stores and anticipated the annual Christmas box which would give them a glimpse into the civilized world Aunt Emma called Boston.

In return letters to their aunt and uncle, the family tried to relate they had a good life in the rural west. They wrote there was a gravel road past their farm, the postman came every day and the rural school was in the next section. They described the school as a modern wooden structure which provided every advantage known to rural education. The school even had electric lights and the REA would be hooking up the farm homes in the future. On Saturday nights, the family drove into town to sell milk and eggs and buy supplies. The family went to the movies and visited friends. On Sundays, they drove the five miles to worship in their country church. It was a far-cry from the existence Aunt Emma and Uncle Otto portrayed to their friends concerning their impoverished relatives living on the prairie out west.

As the days grew close to Christmas, the children watched the mailbox with apprehension. They feared there would be no gifts this year. Uncle Otto had recently sold his shoe store and was now retired. Aunt Emma wrote he spent his days with his garden, stamp collection and doing some woodworking in the basement now that it was winter. She wrote that Otto enjoyed making things with his new saw and electric tools.

The Saturday afternoon before Christmas, the family was busy with the outside chores when they heard the mailman give three beeps with his auto horn. This meant that he had left some mail. Simultaneously, kids came running from the chicken house, pig house and barn. They raced toward the mailbox at the end of the snowy lane. There it sat under the mailbox in the snow! It was almost like an orange crate except it was solid on all sides and of much finer construction. The mysterious box assured the family they would have a good Christmas. Aunt Emma had printed the address: "Mr. and Mrs. Henry Dahlmeyer and family," RFD, Sioux Valley, SD. The postmark was "Boston." The Christmas box had arrived.

The next few days seemed endless. The children conjured up visions of what the large box actually contained. The box was placed under the Christmas tree so it was an exciting thing to contemplate. They knew there would be a gift for each one but the mystery of what those gifts might be was almost more than they could fathom. The older children were in school during the day and baby Carrie was too young to know about Christmas but four-year-old Danny spent his days at home and became closely attached to the gift package. The box had been sanded smooth and it smelled like the pine trees in the backyard, Danny thought. When mother wasn't looking, Danny sat on the box. On one occasion when mother was upstairs, he stood on it and jumped off. What fun!

Christmas Eve finally arrived. The church service was beautiful but the children were anxious to get home and open the box. The candles were lit on the Christmas tree and then blown out again for fear of fire; finally, the box was brought beside the warm coal heater. Mother sat on a stool in front of the package and the children sat or stood around. Dad had brought a screwdriver from the shed and carefully removed the nails which held the lid.

At last the cover was off! The contents were swathed in white tissue paper interspersed with hand knit mittens and scarves. These items, which Aunt Emma knit all year long for her "Dakota family," made good packing for the gifts.

There were two identical gifts on the very top. One had Molly's name and the other was labeled for Edna. Mother gingerly handed the girls their packages. Unwrapping the gifts, the girls found identical dolls with the exception of the dresses. Molly's doll was dressed in pink and Edna's doll was garbed in light blue. The dolls had china heads and eyes which opened and shut. These beautiful dolls were exactly what the girls had wished for. How could Aunt Emma have known?

The next package was smaller but wrapped in much tissue. It was labeled "Agnes." Agnes was 15-years-old and really dreamed of a gift more exciting to her than a doll. Upon removing the layers of packing and a blue scarf which was entwined around it, she found a music box. She opened the door and it tinkled a soft melody. The china lid was covered with painted flowers and leaves spilled down the sides. Such a gift Agnes never imagined!

As mother unpacked the gifts and papa sat by in pleased composure, mother laid the scarves and mittens on the table and indicated, "We'll try them on later."

Next the box revealed a hard, circular package with Harry's name. Harry was eight and had hoped for a horse but it was a small toy train attached to a metal circular track. Wind the train and it ran around the track through a tunnel and into a train station. Pull a lever and the train would stop. Pa remarked, "What will they think of next?"

A square, hard package was labeled for Charlie who was six-years-old. It turned out to be a fascinating Jack-in-the-box. Charlie turned the handle on the side and a funny clown jumped out and almost frightened the little children. The clown was shoved back into the box, the cover closed and Charlie turned the handle again for a repeat performance. Everyone laughed. Charlie loved it.

There was a pair of gloves for papa and a silk scarf for mother. With such fine quality, they would be used only for church going.

The box was nearly empty and wide-eyed Danny was squashed tightly against his mother as he peered eagerly into the bottom contents. When would his gift appear?

Next was a gift with Carrie's name attached. Carrie was the baby and only eight months old but she would soon be old enough to enjoy the caramel colored teddy bear with the brown glass eyes. Mother unwrapped it. Carrie was in her buggy and mother laid the bear in her arms.

The box was empty! Where was Danny's gift? Had Aunt Emma forgotten this four-year-old? The truth hit the group simultaneously and it was a devastating thought! No gift for Danny? Just then mother regained her composure. She picked up the empty box which Uncle Otto had so lovingly built as a crate for the gifts. She presented it to Danny with a big reassuring smile and said, "The box is for Danny!" Danny was immediately laughing and shouting.

He quickly stuffed all the tissue paper into the box and jumped up and down on it. He sat in the bottom and stretched out his little legs as far as possible. He squatted in it and tried to put the cover over the top. He was the happiest kid of all. He could jump off of it and he could sit on it. He could do more with his gift than the rest could do with their presents.

Today Danny lives in Boston and is a very successful businessman. He still prizes his Christmas box.

Now Available!
Signed prints of artwork from "When Coffee Was a Nickel" by nationally-known illustrator Barbara Coppock.

We were overwhelmed by the response to the fine illustrations featured in "When Coffee Was a Nickel." Now, through the cooperation of Barbara Coppock, we have reproduced four of the most popular illustrations from the book.

The illustrations are faithfully rendered on museum quality ivory art paper from the original pencil drawings by the artist. Every line detail and nuance of shading is clearly reproduced in these 10 x 12 inch artist signed prints. Quantities are limited, so order today!

These prints are available individually for $10.00 each. Or, take advantage of our specially priced groupings. Use the order form below. You can also order your friends copies of "When Coffee Was a Nickel."

Quan.	Description	Price
	"April Fool in Country School" $10.00 each	
	"A Country Charivari" $10.00 each	
	"Homeless Hobos" $10.00 each	
	"Harold Goes to School" $10.00 each	
	Schoolhouse Set, one copy each of "April Fool..." and "Harold Goes..." Specially priced at $15.00	
	Complete set of four fine prints You get the fourth print FREE! Only $30.00 for the set of four	
	"When Coffee Was a Nickel" book Publisher's Discount, $8.00!	
	Subtotal	
	S.D. residents add 6% sales tax	
	$3.00 Shipping & Handling	
	Grand Total	

Send check or money order to:
Rushmore House Publishing
Box 1591
Sioux Falls, SD 57101
(605) 334-5253